Engaging with Carol Bacchi

Engaging with Carol Bacchi

Strategic Interventions and Exchanges

edited by

Angelique Bletsas

&

Chris Beasley

Published in Adelaide by

University of Adelaide Press
The University of Adelaide
Level 1, 230 North Terrace
South Australia
5005
press@adelaide.edu.au
www.adelaide.edu.au/press

The University of Adelaide Press publishes externally refereed scholarly books by staff of the University of Adelaide. It aims to maximise the accessibility to its best research by publishing works through the internet as free downloads and as high quality printed volumes on demand.

Electronic Index: this book is available from the website as a down-loadable PDF with fully searchable text. Please use the electronic version to serve as the index.

© 2012 The Authors

This book is copyright. Apart from any fair dealing for the purposes of private study, research, criticism or review as permitted under the *Copyright Act 1968* (Cth), no part may be reproduced, stored in a retrieval system, or transmitted, in any form or by any means, electronic, mechanical, photocopying, recording or otherwise without prior written permission. Address all inquiries to the Director at the above address.

For the full Cataloguing-in-Publication data please contact the National Library of Australia: cip@nla.gov.au

Engaging with Carol Bacchi: strategic interventions and exchanges / edited by Angelique Bletsas, Christine Beasley.

I	Bacchi, Carol Lee, 1948-
II	Women
III	Women—Research

1. Bletsas, Angelique
2. Beasley, Christine

ISBN (electronic) 978-0-9871718-5-6
ISBN (paperback) 978-0-9871718-6-3

Project Editor: Patrick Allington
Cover design: Emma Spoehr
Cover image: © Scout Cuomo http://www.etsy.com/shop/scoutcuomo
Book design: Zoë Stokes

Contents

Acknowledgements　vii

List of Contributors　viii

Introduction　1
Angelique Bletsas and Chris Beasley

Part I　Looking back: On beginning

1　From women's history to women's policy: Pathways and partnerships　9
　Alison Mackinnon

Part II　Strategic interventions and exchanges: Reflections and applications of the '*What's the Problem Represented to be?*' approach

2　Introducing the '*What's the Problem Represented to be?*' approach　21
　Carol Bacchi

Reflections

3　*Women, Policy and Politics*: Recasting policy studies　25
　Susan Goodwin

4　Spaces between: Elaborating the theoretical underpinnings of the '*WPR*'　37
　approach and its significance for contemporary scholarship
　Angelique Bletsas

| 5 | Digging deeper: The challenge of problematising 'inclusive development' and 'disability mainstreaming'
Nina Marshall | 53 |

Applications

6	Answering Bacchi: A conversation about the work and impact of Carol Bacchi in teaching, research and practice in public health *John Coveney and Christine Putland*	71
7	Located subjects: The daily lives of policy workers *Zoë Gill*	79
	Additional interventions: Select reading list	95

Part III   Strategic exchanges: The wider context

| 8 | Making politics fleshly: The ethic of social flesh
Chris Beasley and Carol Bacchi | 99 |
| 9 | Post-structural comparative politics: Acknowledging the political effects of research
Malin Rönnblom | 121 |

Part IV   Looking forward: Still engaged

| 10 | Strategic interventions and ontological politics: Research as political practice
Carol Bacchi | 141 |

Acknowledgements

Angelique Bletsas and Chris Beasley would like to acknowledge the support of the Fay Gale Centre for Research on Gender at The University of Adelaide, South Australia, in initially organising the conference upon which this book is based, and encouraging and assisting with the development of this volume.

List of Contributors

Carol Bacchi is Professor Emerita of Politics at The University of Adelaide. She has taught and researched for over 30 years in history and politics, focusing in particular on feminist theory and policy studies. This volume commemorates and expands upon her work.

Chris Beasley is Reader in Politics and co-Director of the Fay Gale Centre for Research on Gender at The University of Adelaide in South Australia. Her most recent books include *Heterosexuality in Theory and Practice* (Routledge 2012), *Gender and Sexuality: Critical theories, critical thinkers* (Sage 2005) and *What is Feminism?* (Sage 1999). She is currently in the process of writing a seventh book titled, *The Cultural Politics of Popular Film: Power, culture and society* (Manchester UP). Dr Beasley is also engaged in a range of research projects including respectively, critical thinking in the first year university experience, embodied global ethics, migration and masculinities, innovations in heterosexuality and hetero-masculinity, reproductive 'choices' in the context of work/life balance, and the gendered implications of preventive dental health.

Angelique Bletsas was awarded her PhD from The University of Adelaide where she has worked as a lecturer in the Discipline of Politics and the Discipline of Gender, Work, and Social Inquiry. Her primary focus of research has been in the field of welfare policy, but her academic interests span critical policy analysis, governmentality studies, feminist and post-structuralist theories, and higher education policy and practice. She is currently a Research Fellow at the Centre for Work + Life, University of South Australia.

John Coveney is Professor in the Discipline of Public Health, School of Medicine, Flinders University, Adelaide, South Australia. He has professional experience and academic interests that span public health, social science, and the humanities. He has worked in clinical nutrition, and community and public health in Papua New Guinea, Australia and UK. His teaching and research includes public health nutrition, food policy, and health promotion. Professor Coveney has written and co-authored over 120 publications, including books, book chapters, articles and peer-reviewed papers. John is a Research Fellow in The Department of Health Management and Food Policy, City University, London, UK.

Zoë Gill is a Senior Project Officer in the South Australian Department for Health and Ageing and was previously Manager, Research Services, South Australian Parliament Research Library. She has a PhD in Politics and Bachelor of Laws from The University of Adelaide. Her co-authored chapter on policy workers (with Hal Colebatch) appeared in *Beyond the Policy Cycle: The policy process in Australia* and her article on boys' education appeared in *The Australian Educational Researcher*.

Susan Goodwin is Associate Professor in Policy Studies at the University of Sydney. Her research focuses on gender, social policy, and governing through community. She is co-author of the books *The Sociological Bent: Inside metro culture* (Thomson Learning 2005) and *Social Policy for Social Change* (Palgrave Macmillan 2010) and co-editor of *The Good Mother: Contemporary motherhoods in Australia* (Sydney UP 2010) and *Schools, Communities and Social Inclusion* (Palgrave Macmillan 2011). Her work is concerned with the representation of policy issues and methods for accessing representations.

Alison Mackinnon AM is Professor Emerita at the University of South Australia and a Fellow of the Academy of the Social Sciences in Australia. Her extensive publications on women, education, and the changing life course include the prize winning *Love and Freedom: Professional women and the reshaping of personal life* (CUP 1997) and more recently *Women, Love and Learning: The double bind* (Peter Lang 2010). She has held fellowships at Rutgers University, Harvard Graduate School of Education, Newnham College Cambridge, Umeå University, and the Australian National University.

Nina Marshall is a doctoral candidate at the School of Sociology, Politics and International Studies, University of Bristol, UK. Her thesis focuses on the problematisation of disability in international development policy, with particular reference to inclusive development policy by multilateral and bilateral donor organisations.

Christine Putland is Senior Lecturer, Southgate Institute for Health, Society and Equity, Flinders University, Adelaide, South Australia. Christine Putland's background spans community arts, public and social policy, and public health fields. She worked in policy development and management of community services for local government and non-government agencies until joining the Department of Public Health at Flinders University as manager of a research consultancy in 1994. She completed her PhD with Flinders Institute of Public Policy and Management in 1999, and taught in the Graduate Programs in Public Health and Primary Health Care until moving into independent consulting in 2007. Since then Christine has focused on research and evaluation of public health initiatives, specialising in analysis of 'Arts and Health'. She retains academic status with the Southgate Institute for Health, Society and Equity, and continues to publish for both academic and practitioner readers.

Malin Rönnblom has a PhD in Political Science and is Senior Lecturer at the Umeå Centre for Gender Studies, Umeå University, Sweden. Her main research field is policy studies, especially gender equality policy and regional policy and she is also interested in issues of feminist methodology and feminist theory. Rönnblom is senior editor of *NORA - Nordic Journal of Feminist and Gender Research* - and chair of the Swedish Association for Gender Studies. Her recent publications in English include: 'Bending Towards Growth - Discursive constructions of gender equality in an era of governance and neo-liberalism' in Lombardo et al. *Stretching and Bending Gender Equality: Towards an Understanding of Discursive Politics* (Routledge 2009) and 'De-politicising Gender? Constructions of gender equality in Swedish regional policy' in a book she co-edited with Eva Magnusson and Harriet Silius: *Critical Studies of Gender Equalities: Nordic dislocations, dilemmas and contradictions* (Makadam 2008).

Introduction

ANGELIQUE BLETSAS AND CHRIS BEASLEY

Carol Bacchi's scholarship is both substantial and wide-ranging. Beginning her academic career as a historian in the field of English-Canadian women's suffrage, Bacchi has made innovative and insightful contributions to the fields of feminist theory, critical policy studies, and post-structuralist theory. One of the characteristic traits of her scholarship is her interest in revising and revisiting analytic problems from a range of perspectives. To mention just one area in which this is so—the issue of gender difference—Bacchi has explored the use of 'identity' categories in (specifically) gender politics (1996); drawn attention to the way the construction of difference is enacted as a political attribution (2001) and, more recently with collaborator and friend Joan Eveline (2010), put forward the proposition that we ought to conceptualise gender as a verb: an activity or process, rather than as a noun. In each of these projects she has offered a new way to think the 'problem' of identity categories and 'difference' which long preoccupied, and, indeed, frustrated, feminist scholars. The persistence and imagination that is highlighted by this willingness to review and rework key analytical themes and issues is reflective of the tenacity and commitment Bacchi exhibits as a scholar and intellectual.

This resolute analytical rigour is undoubtedly evident in Bacchi's *'What's the Problem Represented to be?'* (*'WPR'*) approach, which is perhaps her most crucial contribution to intellectual inquiry and certainly one of the most innovative analytical frameworks developed in recent times. It is a remarkable tool for investigating a variety of social issues and responses to those issues, and on these grounds forms the greater part of the focus of this book. The *'WPR'* approach offers both an original methodology and scholarly paradigm, by providing to the social sciences a mode of critical enquiry which simultaneously engages to contemporary post-structuralist accounts of power, subjects and social change. This book illuminates, commemorates, and builds upon Bacchi's *'WPR'* approach. It outlines the trajectory of the development of the *'WPR'* approach from Bacchi's early engagements with feminist thinking, as an academic in scholarly environments which were often the preserve of men, towards the theoretical sophistication of an approach which requires an ongoing critical assessment of assumptions about the social world, social 'problems', policy agendas deemed to respond to those 'problems', and the researcher's positioning.

This book arose out of a conference organised by the Fay Gale Centre for Research on Gender at The University of Adelaide honouring Carol Bacchi's work and is intended to make that work accessible to a range of audiences. The conference and book specifically aim to provide an embodied and historically contextualised account of the development of the '*WPR*' approach, rather than seeing this scholarship as arising parthenogenetically, as if from nowhere. In keeping with Bacchi's approach, her work is described here as arising out of a contingent and fleshly sociality.

This contextualised presentation of the development of the '*WPR*' approach follows Bacchi's initial focus on gender and policy, to a wider engagement with the field of policy studies, to a post-positivist concern with theoretically informed applications regarding specific case studies and then to a broader interest in policy as a means to exploring governmentality and governance. In the process Bacchi moved from the shorthand '*What's the Problem*' to an expanded abbreviation '*WPR*' to describe the '*What's the Problem Represented to be?*' approach. This expanded acronym emphasised that her concern was not merely to query how social questions become named and shaped as social problems but to consider more thoroughly the process of problematisation in research, policy and practical applications, as well as the impact of that problematising process. Here Bacchi draws attention to how policy solutions are constituted by the assumptions entailed in the problematising process, rather than being self-evidently responsive to objective social 'problems'.

As Carol Bacchi herself notes (Chapter 2, Part 2), the emphasis upon 'problem' *questioning*, as against policy solutions, in the '*WPR*' approach provides an open-ended mode of critical practice, enabling rigorous and trenchant appraisal of policy agendas—especially those that seem axiomatic or patently obvious. Yet, this approach is by no means limited to policy analysis alone. This is an approach which can serve to investigate the specific particularities of policies but can also be readily employed in examination of modes of measurement, cultural materials, social debates, economic decision-making, and so on. In this context, a crucial aspect of the '*WPR*' approach as a mode of critical practice is also to highlight the politics of research, to recognise that research methods and reports are by no means neutral but rather are always political acts with social effects. Indeed, Bacchi's work is driven by her commitment to developing 'practical' useful theorising which can bring to the fore the political character of research. Such an orientation is certainly especially evident in relation to the '*WPR*' approach. Bacchi, while working on her book *Women, Policy and Politics* (1999), which articulated an initial account of the approach, presented seminars to the South Australian state government Office for the Status of Women and Health Department with the aim of investigating whether it would make sense to policy workers. The success of these seminars convinced Bacchi that the '*WPR*' approach could be of use in interrogating taken-for-granted policy premises, even amongst those who might be strongly wedded to particular policy agendas. Since then she has actively sought out a range of further opportunities for employing the approach which might extend its practical applications. The evolution of the '*WPR*' approach and its methodological apparatus has undoubtedly contributed to its increasing breadth of application and portability, as will become evident in the organisation of this book.

The structure of the book largely follows the trajectory of Bacchi's body of work. The four parts plot a path from the early points of inquiry which fired Bacchi's scholarship—the personal and theoretical interrogation of, specifically, *gender* politics inside and outside of the academe—to the revisioning and revaluing of key tenets fundamental to the field of political studies which informs her more recent study.

Part 1 is thus concerned with 'Beginnings'. In Chapter 1 Alison Mackinnon, a historian and long-time friend of Carol's, provides the engaging story of their initial entry into academia, as well as detailing Bacchi's subsequent contributions to the fields of history and politics. Mackinnon's conversational narrative provides a rare insight into the pioneering first steps of an early generation of female academics and activists who did not just struggle to take their place in the academe, but to reconstitute it. The experience of women in university institutions is a crucial initial theme in the development of Bacchi's research agenda.

Part 2, 'Strategic interventions and exchanges: Reflections and applications of the "*What's the Problem Represented to be?*" approach' is dedicated to an analysis, elaboration, and critical extension of the '*WPR*' approach. The chapters in Part 2 demonstrate why the '*WPR*' approach has had such a profound and lasting impact on the field of policy studies. For readers unfamiliar with the approach, or those who may find it useful to have a convenient shorthand version of its key presuppositions, Part 2 begins with an overview of the '*WPR*' approach from Carol Bacchi (Chapter 2). The overview details the analytical maturing of the approach and outlines the key themes of the '*WPR*' methodology. The six all-important questions which make up the '*WPR*' approach are also provided here.

The next three chapters all serve as 'reflections' on Bacchi's '*WPR*' approach. In Chapter 3, '*Women, Policy and Politics*: Recasting policy studies', Susan Goodwin locates Bacchi's '*WPR*' approach in the field of policy studies and explores her own engagement with how the approach works to transform the conventional narrative of policy studies. Goodwin draws attention to the special efficacy of the '*WPR*' approach as a methodology and the way it allows policy analysts to not only critically assess policy proposals, but also to make transparent the ways in which they arrive at their conclusions. Goodwin argues that, by allowing analysts to show how they arrive at their assessment of a given policy proposal, the '*WPR*' approach rescues their work from charges of partisan bias.

In Chapter 4 Angelique Bletsas explicates the theoretical framework underlying the '*WPR*' approach. She demonstrates the way in which the approach facilitates a critical questioning of the 'problem solving paradigm' argued to dominate contemporary approaches to policy analysis and policy making. Specifically, Bletsas illustrates the way the critical orientation underlying Bacchi's '*WPR*' approach enables new critical interventions in the fields of poverty and welfare policy.

Nina Marshall in Chapter 5 extends this reflection on Bacchi's '*WPR*' approach, raising critical questions as to whether, as a mode of thinking, the approach can be reconciled with strategic interventions in the disability sector. Marshall's area of research is in the nascent field of disability-in-development and her contribution offers new thinking on how the '*WPR*' approach can be wedded to activist politics and on how we define policy texts.

Chapters 6 and 7 both offer 'applications' of the '*WPR*' approach, further highlighting its usefulness. In Chapter 6 John Coveney and Christine Putland reflect on their engagement with the approach and the way it has served as a strategic pedagogical tool to highlight the assumptions of public health policy for students who were accustomed to a positivist framing of health issues as simply reflective of an objective reality.

Chapter 7, by Zoë Gill, presents a shift in focus, from discussing the ways in which the '*WPR*' approach recasts orthodox understandings of policy analysis, to investigating the policy making process as it is implicitly constituted in policy makers self-understandings. Gill advances an innovative and insightful analysis of the way policy makers understand themselves as particular kinds of actors. She argues that, implicit in these understandings, is a particular pre-existent account of the policy making process as developing an evidence-based solution to an objective problem. Here, application of the '*WPR*' approach may be viewed as a challenging intervention in the self-definition of policy makers.

As the relevance of Bacchi's '*WPR*' approach continues to be discovered by theorists and practitioners working in diverse fields, Part 2 concludes with a short reference list of additional 'interventions' which employ the '*WPR*' approach. The reference list is intended as a guide for readers interested in further pursuing existing applications of Bacchi's '*WPR*' approach.

The chapters in Part 3, 'Strategic exchanges: The wider context', present a more expansive analytic focus and move beyond the strategic interventions into policy which the '*WPR*' approach facilitates. Both chapters in Part 3 are, in different ways, the product of an 'exchange' of ideas in a direct sense. Chapter 8 is co-authored by Chris Beasley and Carol Bacchi who have had a long and fruitful intellectual collaboration. Chapter 9, by Malin Rönnblom, is similarly an example of an exchange of ideas, as Rönnblom employs the '*WPR*' approach as a means of advancing inquiry in her own field of comparative politics. Importantly, the chapters in Part 3 can be understood to involve some element of strategic encounter in a further sense, as both address the question of how implications—'effects'— arise, not just from *how* research is carried out (a key theme of the '*WPR*' approach), but from what comes to be taken for granted, and what excluded, from any given research framework. More to the point, both are concerned to highlight how an 'exchange' of ideas in our research categories can change the shape and scope of our analytical and political projects.

In Chapter 8, 'Making politics fleshly: The ethics of social flesh', Chris Beasley and Carol Bacchi reflect on their work on social interconnection, arguing that approaches attending to interconnection, such as citizenship, democratic and social movement theorising, as well as terms like trust, respect, care and responsibility, are significantly limited by their failure to attend adequately to *bodies*. They set out a re-theorisation of social relations as 'social flesh'.

In Chapter 9 Malin Rönnblom also engages the theme of research frameworks, offering a critique and novel reconceptualisation of the field of comparative politics. Where Beasley and Bacchi address a failure to attend to the material of bodies in thinking about social relations and intersubjectivity, Rönnblom argues that contemporary comparative politics suffers the inverse problem: mistaking its concepts and categories of analysis for pre-given materialities. Though they therefore pursue different analytic ends, both chapters highlight the political implications of taken-for-granted terms of scholarship, a prominent theme in the book.

In lieu of a separate editorial conclusion we considered that, given the focus of the book, the last word in this publication should be provided by Bacchi herself. Thus we include in Part 4, titled 'Looking forward', a new work by Carol Bacchi. Despite her retirement in 2009, her scholarship continues to develop in new directions. Appropriately, therefore, the final chapter, Chapter 10, is not a reflection on what has been, but a call to action as to what might yet come to be—a critical and strategic reimagining of research practice as 'ontological politics'. Consistent with Bacchi's enduring commitment to keeping the politics of scholarship and knowledge central to research practice, Chapter 10, 'Strategic interventions and ontological politics: Research as political practice', serves as a new contemplation and articulation of the ways in which research interventions, strategic and otherwise, have political effects.

For Bacchi, research is never *simply* descriptive of a 'problem' or issue, it always signals a politics, and this is a key theme of each of the chapters presented in this volume. This interest in the effects of research frameworks and the interventions that flow from them, should remind us that the political nature of research practice creates a responsibility for us as scholars, policy makers, researchers and students to be attentive to what we include and what we exclude in the visions we draw of social life. Yet, we should remember too that the political effects of research practice, which always proliferate in ways which exceed our intentions, also enable the opportunity for new and unexpected exchanges—with ideas, with the world, and with each other. After all, the lasting contribution of Bacchi's scholarship, which this book is designed to reflect, arises not only from recognition of the importance of new thought and how its application to old 'problems' creates possibilities for positive change. In other words, our concern is not only with the importance of 'strategic interventions'. The lasting contribution of Bacchi's scholarship also arises from the recognition of the need for exchange, collaboration, and partnership. Exchange improves our research practice, and, when we are truly fortunate, it also enriches our lives. Certainly, we have both been enriched by our collaborative ventures and exchanges with Carol Bacchi and her work. We offer this book in the hope that other researchers can likewise benefit from the groundbreaking work of a unique thinker and a much valued friend.

Part I

Looking back: On beginning

1 | From women's history to women's policy: Pathways and partnerships

ALISON MACKINNON

A personal reflection

My links with Carol Bacchi go back a long way, probably much further back than either of us cares to admit. Carol started teaching at The University of Adelaide in the History Department in 1978 as a tutor in Australian history. I was teaching in what was then the Education Department as a tutor in the history of education. Perhaps I need to explain here exactly what a tutor was, as it is a species that is now virtually extinct in Australia. Tutors, mainly women, took tutorial classes—usually six to eight a week—attended lectures and undertook vast stacks of marking. They were also meant to complete their higher degrees if they had not done so already, and to engage in research. There was no guarantee that a tutoring job would lead to anything else but somehow Carol and I managed to move on to academic posts. As a mother of three young children at the time, I thought tutoring was a dream job and I fervently hoped to keep it for life. But that was before the women's movement fired up my ambition. I am sure neither of us would have thought in our wildest dreams that we would become professors—generally women did not.

We met up in the 1980s in the context of the various working groups that gathered to challenge the very low position of women at The University of Adelaide. That challenge was ultimately successful in improving conditions for women and in creating the Women's Studies Research Centre—a forerunner of the current Fay Gale Centre for Research on Gender, the host for the conference which led to this volume. Incidentally, the late Professor Fay Gale was also a major force in that battle and, as our first female professor, took the struggle to the highest levels within the university. So that is when we met—Carol having finished a PhD on English-Canadian women's suffrage in 1976, and me researching a PhD on the earliest

Here we are with our friend Ngaire Naffine.

women university graduates and their life patterns. We were both keen advocates of women's history. Carol's thesis on the ideology of the Canadian women's suffrage movement became her first book *Liberation Deferred? The ideas of the English-Canadian suffragists* (University of Toronto Press) first published in 1983. My first book *One Foot on the Ladder* came out in 1984; so we were keen young academic historians, inspired by the women's movement and keen to change the world.

What was the world like in 1983? We listened to the Beach Boys, Simon and Garfunkel and Diana Ross. Madonna brought out her first album (my goodness, has she been around that long?) and Michael Jackson produced his 'Thriller' video clip. Bob Hawke was elected Australian Prime Minister, Sally Ride was the first American woman in space and Australia won the America's Cup. They were heady days! Somewhere around that time I went with Carol and her then husband Fred to the original Leonard Cohen concert at the Adelaide Festival Centre—and I mean the original concert, not one of the many repeats. We were also very intrepid in those days! Carol and I walked and talked all through the Adelaide Hills as we trained to go trekking in Nepal in 1986. But enough of this frivolous stuff.

We were serious students of the academic world, particularly as it applied to women, and we met regularly to discuss articles and ideas. I am now going to mention something that Carol currently reflects on with some amusement. One day she said to me, with a puzzled look

(I can't date this exactly), 'Alison, what exactly is all this "theory"?' So we started to talk about theory and to read about theory and of course at that time that meant Foucault. That led to our first article together 'Sex, resistance and power: sex reform in South Australia c 1905', which was published in *Australian Historical Studies* in April 1988. Here we demonstrated that we knew our Foucault while discussing the fascinating case of the Adelaide early twentieth-century sex reformers Rosamond Benham and her mother Angus Nesbit Benham. We were particularly interested in issues of power, a key concern in 1980s feminist thinking. We took on, in particular, Foucault's notion of refusing to identify protagonists in the struggle for power: 'I would say it's all against all', Foucault claimed. 'Who fights against whom? We all fight each other.' He also spoke of 'an intermingling of resistance of power so complete that one cannot talk of victories and defeats' (1980: 208).

Carol and Alison at Lukla 'airport', Nepal.

We took issue with this analysis. 'This type of analysis underestimates the importance of the fact that some protagonists have more power at their disposal than others', we wrote, 'and that this distribution of power will affect the shape that resistance takes. It also makes it difficult to examine changes in power relations'. 'Our concern', we argued, 'is *the relative power of men and women, and their potential to challenge the structures which shape them*' (Mackinnon and Bacchi 1988: 61, emphasis added).

I will not go into any more detail about that article. It was a great pleasure to work with Carol on it and on a later piece we wrote together in 1991 for the US journal *Genders*. But it strikes me in rereading those words that in some way they could stand as a manifesto for Carol's later work—a concern with the relative power of men and women and their potential to challenge the structures that shape them. In looking back we can often trace the continuities in our working lives. In what follows I briefly trace some of the journeys we have taken since those early days and then I will consider in particular continuities in Carol's body of work and above all her magnificent contribution to challenging the structures that shape women's lives. But first a small detour.

The double bind

It is not surprising that having taught in a school of education I continue to be fascinated by the importance of education, particularly the struggles for women to achieve an education equal to that of men. I have an abiding interest therefore in the lives of women who graduate from universities and who then negotiate in differing contexts lives that include rewarding professional careers and equally rewarding personal lives with partners and possibly children. In an earlier book I described this as a challenge between love and freedom, those words really standing as proxies for autonomy and commitment (Mackinnon 1997). My most recent book is titled *Women, Love and Learning: the double bind* and I revisit those same dilemmas through the lens of a later generation, women who graduated in the 1950s and early 60s in Australia and the US (Mackinnon 2010). Those were conservative years (have you been watching the TV series *Mad Men*?) and women who attended universities (or 'colleges' as those institutions giving undergraduate degrees were called in the US) were expected to marry early, produce several children and support their husband's careers. There were a few outliers who managed to build careers and escape too obvious discrimination but they kept their heads down on the whole, lucky to be accepted at all much less to think about making a fuss.

But some graduates from that period did refuse to accept a lesser role—think Germaine Greer and Gloria Steinem, not to mention our own trail blazing Fay Gale and Anne Levy. They struggled with the contradictions of the time, taking seriously the claims of their education and refusing to put it all aside. They began to challenge the structures that shaped them. Later, following their lead, women's historians such as Carol and me and many others began to fill in women's missing past. Working in universities we began to see very clearly the inequities still remaining—the 'double bind' women faced if they wished to build successful careers in an institution clearly shaped by and for men. With many other like-minded women we both worked for change through university committees and also through an analysis of what the 'problems' were. Here, like so many other women in academia at that time, we were undertaking research very specifically as political practice with an overt agenda of change.

Framing the problem: Same difference

One of the defining questions that shaped much inquiry at the time was this: were women the same as or different from men? How then could women frame their demands for more equitable treatment? We can begin to trace a continuity here in Carol's work—a concern with how demands are framed and the critical importance of the language of that framing to the outcome. In her earlier work on the English-Canadian suffragists Carol had examined how women in Canada came to frame their demand for enfranchisement given their specific historical, cultural and political locations. The question of sameness and difference was so critical in framing the thinking of the late eighties that Carol devoted a major book to it— one of her first strategic interventions. (I'm very proud of this book and I was delighted to see when I opened it again after many years that it was dedicated to five people, one of whom was me.) *Same Difference: feminism and sexual difference*, published in 1990, marked Carol's transition from history to politics. Yet it also had a strong historical dimension. Carol's background as an historian has given her an important ability to acknowledge the historical circumstances in which particular debates occur and in which particular changes are possible. *Same Difference* takes as its point of departure the way in which different groups within the women's movement between the wars struggled to find a space to articulate forms of change that would assist women past the 'double bind'. The second half of the book follows this topic into late twentieth-century feminist debates around some key public policy issues, including paid maternity leave and anti-discrimination law.

Interestingly, one of the epigraph quotations is from Wittgenstein and I quote, in part:

> But if anyone believes that certain concepts are absolutely the correct ones, and that having different ones would mean not realizing something that we realize—then let him imagine certain very general facts of nature to be different from what we are used to, and the formation of concepts different from the usual ones will become intelligible to him. (Wittgenstein, in Bacchi 1990, epigraph)

Here we already see a source of Carol's ongoing fascination with concepts as they stand, their ability to define, and how they might be changed or re-imagined. This is a continuing theme in her work.

Following *Same Difference*, Carol tackled the key question of affirmative action and the politics surrounding the debates on the subject in her book *The Politics of Affirmative Action* (Sage 1996). The book reported on her major research project, examining affirmative action theory and practice in six countries that were purportedly leading the world in affirmative action. Again Carol focused on the language used and 'the ways in which the concepts and categories used in political debate are constructed and deployed for political purposes' (xi). As she explained in the introduction 'I have coined the term "category politics" to talk about the ways in which categories figure in affirmative action debates' (xi). The book goes on to examine the political uses of both conceptual and identity categories in affirmative action theory and practice. From this perspective Carol argued that *we can thus recognise political and other social theorists as political actors*—a key argument of the book (xi) and of the conference held in Carol's honour in 2010, which inspired this volume. Again, in examining the specific arguments in particular countries such as the US or Canada, Carol insists upon the historical specificity that has shaped particular ways of thinking and analysing structures of power.

Carol Bacchi's 1999 book *Women, Policy and Politics* follows logically from her earlier work. It develops a particular view about the way in which policies are constructed. She argues, in sum,

> that governments, and indeed all of us, *give a particular shape* to social 'problems' in the ways in which we speak about them and in the proposals we advance to 'address' them. Governments in this understanding are active in the *creation* of particular ways of understanding issues. I call competing understandings of social issues 'problem representations' and argue that it is crucially important to identify competing problem representations because they constitute a form of political intervention with a range of effects (Bacchi 2007: 1).

This work introduces the '*What is the Problem Represented to be*' ('*WPR*') approach—an important methodological and theoretical advance. I do not intend to discuss this approach in any detail here as several other contributors will do so (see Goodin, Bletsas, Marshall, Gill, this volume). However, in reflecting on that approach I find that I have taken on board some of its features in my own work. For instance, in a recently completed research project titled 'The Utopian Imagination of Young People on the Margins' the research group agonised over the term 'marginalised young people' (Robb et al. 2010). How were they marginalised, these young people who could not function in mainstream schools, who had had brushes with the juvenile justice system? They were certainly not marginal in their own eyes: they were the centre of their own and their peers' universe. Yet in labelling them as marginalised we relegated them to a different status, a lesser status than those in the (self-appointed) centre. By seeing them as central and the margins as a key site of understanding, our thinking about young people's hopes and dreams can be both challenged and enriched.

Carol and Joan: A wonderful partnership

I have talked about my partnership with Carol over the years but now I would like to turn to another very important partnership in Carol's life and career. Carol's 1996 book *The Politics of Affirmative Action* is dedicated 'To Joan' and contains a chapter jointly written with Joan Eveline. On the acknowledgements page Carol writes of Joan's support throughout the writing of the book, stating *inter alia*: 'I have seldom experienced such an exhilarating and productive friendship.' This was an enormously productive relationship that continued over many years and culminated, in a professional sense, with the publication in 2010 of the latest book, *Mainstreaming Politics: gendering practice and feminist theory*, written jointly with Joan.

From women's history to women's policy: Pathways and partnerships | 15

Carol with friend and colleague Joan Eveline.

The book is a clear example of research as political practice: the outcome of an Australian Research Council Linkage research grant which was to design gender analysis procedures for the Western Australian and South Australian public sectors. I would like to acknowledge here the work of Joan Eveline, a dear friend of many in Carol's research community, whose death before that book was finished has left so many people—and the feminist work to which she contributed—so much the poorer. Joan also challenged the conceptual frameworks through which women's lives and work were viewed. One of her many lasting contributions is her reversal of the notion of 'women's disadvantage'. This we should name for what it is, she argued, 'men's advantage' (Eveline 1994). This indeed represented the problem very differently, as lying with men, rather than women, and it challenged men to say why they were entitled to such advantages.

When Joan died the book that became *Mainstreaming Politics* was only partly formed. Although Joan and Carol were able to discuss issues almost to the end of Joan's life they often thought very differently about theory, and a partially completed jointly authored book was a considerable challenge. I believe that Carol's intellectual persistence in completing the book alone, attempting at all times to be true to Joan's ideas and to keep up the sense of a 'dialogue' between them, a major feature of their collaboration, was a true labour of love. This is a deeply reflexive book, the authors generously opening up their ways of thinking and analysing to a wider audience. Here we see writ large the coming to fruition of both Carol's deep interest in post-structural theory (Foucault I notice is there as he was in our earliest article, still with that concern about asymmetrical power relations) and her concern with policy—both in theory and practice. This is a volume rich with insights such as the proposal that 'policies produce or constitute political subjects' (8). There is much in this book for theorists and for practitioners of policy and gender analysis.

Conclusion

In concluding, it has been a fascinating journey for me to look back through a past of over a quarter of a century of knowing Carol and working with her, sometimes quite closely, at other times from a distance as our paths diverged. I have been struck by the continuity of the themes in Carol's work and their increasing theoretical sophistication and policy reach. And that reach is both a national and an international one. As Malin Rönnblom has commented, and as I found out in a recent trip to Sweden, Carol's work is widely known and respected, particularly in Scandinavia and Denmark where engagement with similar issues is deep and current. In Australia, Carol recently was an invited speaker at the Melbourne Writers Festival, surely an accolade of the greatest honour for an author.

I have attempted to link our journeys in some way, as two young women who started out in universities in a very different social and political climate and arrived at destinations we could not have imagined. Maybe that was only a possibility for that particular time and place. Yet I think we would both agree that although the academic world has changed to a remarkable degree since we started out there is still a considerable price to pay for women in academia, particularly women with children. We have both had to reinvent ourselves to fit the category of 'academic', to bring to the fore certain characteristics and to suppress others. I find that as that category begins to unravel—the further one moves from the university, its teaching, its committees and its politics—the more one begins to reclaim a different, more expansive category and identity, at times to reclaim identities that have been forfeited for academic ends, while maintaining some of the passion that motivated us.

Both Carol and I draw on an understanding of history to understand, to define and to seek to change the problems of our time. It is interesting then to see how we fit into the history of women in universities and public life. In my recent book *Women, Love and Learning* I reflected upon an observation by the American scholar Patricia Graham on education for women as a means of exempting them from the 'norms' of their day. Graham argued that in the earliest days of women's education, as the nineteenth century turned into the twentieth, the possession of a degree exempted women from the norms of their time (Mackinnon 2010). Indeed, as I have argued elsewhere, almost half of those earliest women graduates did not marry or have children and forged independent lives, many devoting themselves to issues concerning women. In the mid-twentieth century an undergraduate degree no longer served to exempt women from the norms of their society—it was relatively commonplace. At that time having a higher degree—a doctorate, for instance—or advanced professional qualifications such as a medical specialist might have served to exempt women from the norms. I then reflected on what we would need today to exempt young women from the norms of our society as higher degrees, MBAs and specialist training have become more common, relatively speaking.

It occurs to me in the context of this discussion that what has happened is that the norms themselves have changed immeasurably due to the research, analysis and political action of a generation of feminists who have challenged the concepts open to them, and have introduced new terms to shape issues, terms such as sexual harassment. This is the critical work of our generation and Carol Bacchi is in the forefront of that work, seeking new conceptual frameworks, new modes of analysis and freeing us from the conceptual and linguistic double binds of the past. It is a wonderful contribution.

The concluding chapter of Carol's 1996 book on the politics of affirmative action is titled 'Conclusion: no final curtain'. I feel sure that those words could equally stand for Carol's exit from formal university employment. This is no final curtain, I feel sure. Keep your eyes open for the next enthralling act.

References

Bacchi, C. (1983) *Liberation Deferred? The ideas of the English-Canadian Suffragists*, Toronto: University of Toronto Press.
—— (1990) *Same Difference: Feminism and sexual difference*, Sydney: Allen and Unwin.
—— (1996) *The Politics of Affirmative Action: 'Women', equality and category politics*, London: Sage.
—— (1999) *Women, Policy and Politics: The construction of policy problems*, London: Sage.
—— (2007) 'What's the Problem Represented to be: An introduction'. Available HTTP: <http://www.flinders.edu.au/medicine/fms/sites/southgate/documents/theory%20club/2007-oct/IntroducingWP_Bacchi.pdf> (accessed June 2011).
—— (2009) *Analysing Policy: What's the problem represented to be?* Frenchs Forest, NSW: Pearson Education.
Bacchi, C. and J. Eveline (2010) *Mainstreaming Politics: Gendering practices and feminist theory*, Adelaide: University of Adelaide Press.
Bacchi, C. and A. Mackinnon (1991) 'Re-politicizing gender: a response to Desley Deacon', *Genders*, 11: 126-33.
Eveline, J. (1994) 'The politics of advantage', *Australian Feminist Studies*, Special Issue Women and Citizenship, 19: 129-54.
Foucault, M. (1980) *Power/Knowledge: Selected Interviews and Other Writings, 1972-1977* (ed. C. Gordon), Brighton: Harvester.
Mackinnon, A. (1984) *One Foot on the Ladder: Origins and outcomes of girls' secondary schooling in South Australia*, St Lucia: University of Queensland Press.
—— (1997) *Love and Freedom: Professional women and the reshaping of personal life*, Cambridge:

Cambridge University Press.

—— (2010) *Women, Love and Learning: The double bind*, Bern: Peter Lang.

Mackinnon, A. and C. Bacchi (1988) 'Sex, resistance and power: Sex reform in South Australia c 1905', *Australian Historical Studies*, 23(90): 60-71.

Robb, S., P. O'Leary, A. Mackinnon and P. Bishop (2010) *Hope: The everyday and imaginary worlds of young people on the margins*, Adelaide: Wakefield Press.

Part II

Strategic interventions and exchanges: Reflections and applications of the '*What's the Problem Represented to be?*' approach

2 | Introducing the 'What's the Problem Represented to be?' approach

CAROL BACCHI

The '*WPR*' approach is a resource, or tool, intended to facilitate critical interrogation of public policies. It starts from the premise that what one proposes to do about something reveals what one thinks is problematic (needs to change). Following this thinking, policies and policy proposals contain *implicit* representations of what is considered to be the 'problem' ('problem representations'). For example, if forms of training are recommended to improve women's status and promotion opportunities, the implication is that *their lack of training* is the 'problem', responsible for 'holding them back'. The task in a '*WPR*' analysis is to read policies with an eye to discerning how the 'problem' is represented within them and to subject this problem representation to critical scrutiny. This task is accomplished through a set of six questions and an accompanying undertaking to apply the questions to one's own proposals for change:

1. What's the 'problem' (for example, of 'problem gamblers', 'drug use/abuse', 'gender inequality', 'domestic violence', 'global warming', 'sexual harassment', etc.) represented to be in a specific policy or policy proposal?
2. What presuppositions or assumptions underpin this representation of the 'problem'?
3. How has this representation of the 'problem' come about?
4. What is left unproblematic in this problem representation? Where are the silences? Can the 'problem' be thought about differently?
5. What effects are produced by this representation of the 'problem'?
6. How/where has this representation of the 'problem' been produced, disseminated and defended? How has it been (or could it be) questioned, disrupted and replaced?

Apply this list of questions to your own problem representations.

Question 1 assists in clarifying the implicit problem representation within a specific policy or policy proposal. Subsequent questions encourage:

- reflection on the underlying premises in this representation of the 'problem' (Question 2)
- consideration of the contingent practices and processes through which this understanding of the 'problem' has emerged (Question 3)
- careful scrutiny of possible gaps or limitations in this representation of the 'problem', accompanied by inventive imagining of potential alternatives (Question 4)
- considered assessment of how identified problem representations limit what can be talked about as relevant, shape people's understandings of themselves and the issues, and impact materially on people's lives (Question 5)
- a sharpened awareness of the contestation surrounding representation of the 'problem' (Question 6).

The undertaking to apply the six questions to one's own proposals signals a commitment to include oneself and one's thinking as part of the 'material' to be analysed. The argument here is that the ways in which 'problems' are constituted elicit particular forms of subjectivity, influencing how we see ourselves and others. Hence, self-problematisation ('reflexivity') forms a crucial part of the analysis.

In this account policy is not the government's best effort to *solve* 'problems'; rather, policies *produce* 'problems' with particular meanings that affect what gets done or not done, and how people live their lives. However, the focus is not on intentional issue manipulation or strategic framing. Instead, the aim is to understand policy better than policy makers by probing the unexamined assumptions and deep-seated conceptual logics within implicit problem representations. This focus means paying attention to the forms of knowledge that underpin public policies, such as psychological or biomedical premises, producing a broad conception of governing that encompasses the place of experts and professionals.

In this view the 'public', of which we are members, is governed, not through policies, but through problematisations—how 'problems' are constituted. To be clear, this claim does not ignore the host of troubling conditions in people's (and peoples') lives; nor does it suggest that we are simply talking about competing interpretations of those conditions. To the contrary the proposition is that lives are lived in specific ways *due to* the shaping impact of proposals that create particular understandings of 'problems'. Hence the analysis counters a relativist assumption that any one 'truth' is as good as any other.

The '*WPR*' approach has a broad field of application. Specific pieces of legislation or policy pronouncements provide the most obvious starting points for analysis. However, more general government documents also contain implicit problem representations. For example, a stated commitment to 'community cohesion' in a government report implies that there is *a lack of* this presumably desirable state or condition in the community (i.e. lack of community cohesion is constituted as a 'problem'). Governmental instruments, such as censuses or activity regimes for the unemployed, can also be analysed to reveal underlying assumptions about what is problematic and what needs to change. In addition, the '*WPR*' approach facilitates a form of critical thinking that extends well beyond the study of government and public policy. For example, the six questions prove useful in identifying the underlying presuppositions and forms of problematisation in theoretical and methodological propositions, which are in effect postulated 'solutions'.

Initially the approach to policy analysis outlined above was described as the '*What's the Problem?*' approach (Bacchi 1999). It became clear that amplification was needed due to the tendency for some readers to interpret this question to mean a determination to seek out the 'real problem' in order to develop 'appropriate' 'solutions'. The '*WPR*' acronym, shorthand for '*What's the Problem Represented to be?*' (for which I thank Angelique Bletsas), is intended to make it clear that the point of the analysis is to begin with postulated 'solutions', such as policies, in order to tease out and critically examine their implicit problem representations. At the same time, Question 4 opens up a space to imagine different futures but always with a commitment to examine proposals for their modes of problematising.

The most recent incarnation of the '*WPR*' approach (Bacchi 2009) includes two questions (Questions 3 and 6) that did not appear in its initial formulation. The goal in these questions is to develop a sharpened awareness of the forms of power involved in the shaping of problem representations. A genealogical tracing of the emergence of particular forms of problematisation, prompted by Question 3, also highlights the spaces for challenge and change.

These elaborations signal that the '*WPR*' approach ought to be conceived as an open-ended mode of critical engagement, rather than as a formula. In light of this understanding I have recently:

- asked some 'hard questions' concerning the notion of reflexivity (Bacchi 2011)
- probed the analytic potential of the concept 'discursive practices' (Bacchi and Bonham 2011)
- considered more fully the political implications of different analytical paradigms (Bacchi and Rönnblom 2011).

In an era when a problem-*solving* motif is near hegemonic—think here of evidence-based policy and contemporary western eagerness to produce students as 'problem solvers'—the '*WPR*' approach serves as a much needed interruption to the presumption that 'problems' are fixed and uncontroversial starting points for policy development. It reminds us that the banal and vague notion of 'the problem' and its partner 'the solution' are heavily laden with meaning. To probe this meaning the '*WPR*' approach recommends 'problem'-*questioning* as a form of critical practice.

References

Bacchi, C. (1999) *Women, Policy and Politics: The construction of policy problems*, London: Sage.

—— (2009) *Analysing Policy: What's the problem represented to be?* Frenchs Forest: Pearson Education.

—— (2011) 'Gender mainstreaming and reflexivity: Asking some hard questions', keynote address at the Advancing Gender+ Training in Theory and Practice Conference: An international conference for practitioners, experts and commissioners in Gender+ training, Complutense University, Madrid, 3 February.

Bacchi, C. and J. Bonham (2011) 'Reclaiming discursive practices as an analytic focus: political implications', forthcoming.

Bacchi, C. and M. Rönnblom (2011) 'Feminist Discursive Institutionalism—What's Discursive About It? Limitations of conventional political studies paradigms', forthcoming.

3 | *Women, Policy and Politics*: Recasting policy studies

SUSAN GOODWIN

Introduction

Carol Bacchi's book *Women, Policy and Politics: the Construction of Policy Problems,* published in 1999, introduced a powerful new approach to the study of policy which resonated with researchers and practitioners in a wide range of fields, in Australia and internationally. In some ways, the book can be seen as having had a 'matchmaking' role. It comprehensively introduced post-structuralism and social constructionism to policy studies, but it also introduced feminists to alternative ways of conceptualising policy, policy processes and policy analysis. Both of these meetings have been incredibly fruitful. For feminists undertaking research on gender issues, the book provided new perspectives on key areas of concern such as pay equity, abortion, childcare and domestic violence. Scholarship and practice in each of these areas have benefitted from the insights provided in the book. In this chapter, however, I focus predominantly on the implications for the field of policy studies (including, of course, feminist policy studies), arguing that the framework developed in *Women, Policy and Politics*, and expanded and refined in later work, significantly recast the field.

The recasting of policy studies has been an important intervention. As I discuss, policy studies can suffer from an over-emphasis on the technical dimensions of governing, lending it a reputation as a 'dry' field of research and practice, dominated by 'fact-finders' and 'problem solvers'. In contrast, Bacchi's focus on knowledge practices and power relations broadened the appeal of policy analysis, which was presented as a way of participating in politics through the interrogation of how meaning is made. In what follows, I discuss three elements of Bacchi's work that have been important in this recasting. First, I suggest that *Women, Politics and Policy* re-narrated the field of policy studies. In Bacchi's account of the field, policy approaches were distinguished in terms of how they conceptualise social problems rather than along conventional lines, where approaches to policy analysis have been distinguished in terms of how they address, or handle, social problems. This new account thus enabled a discussion of ideas, issues and debates concerning the relationship between policy and 'problems' and forwarded the idea that policy deals with (and constitutes) representations of problems, or problematisations. Thus, in this new narrative, the very objects of policy studies were recast.

Women, Policy and Politics also contributed to the development of reflexive policy analyses. The approach developed in the book, and the examples used to illustrate the approach, encouraged policy analysts to turn their gaze to their own categories of analysis and taken-for-granted presuppositions and beliefs. This kind of reflexivity has proven to be particularly useful in analyses of the framing of 'women's inequality' in policy, but is applicable wherever a critical analysis of policy is deemed to be required. In the final section of the chapter I describe the important contribution *Women, Policy and Politics* made to policy research practice. In the book, Bacchi laid out a methodology for apprehending how meaning is created in policy discourses. Described as the '*What's the Problem Represented to be?*' approach (and in later work as the '*WPR*' approach), this contribution has provided policy researchers with a tool for systematically accessing problem representations in policy. The methodology involves a range of strategies, including discourse analysis, genealogical analysis and archaeological analysis. While these kinds of analytic strategies are often associated with quite complex theory, there is a straight-forwardness about the '*What's the Problem Represented to be?*' approach that has rendered it accessible and widely applicable. A key contribution of the chapter is my suggestion that providing a methodology for analysing policy as discourse has been significant for both the practice of policy research *and* the politics of policy practice.

Recasting the field of policy studies

Policy studies is a field of practice, rather than a discipline. Those who populate the field include historians, sociologists, political scientists, philosophers as well as researchers and practitioners from social policy, public administration, public policy and gender and cultural studies. Over the decades, a range of different conceptual schemas have been employed to make sense of the field. Common distinctions include the identification of approaches as 'traditional' or 'rationalist', which are contrasted with approaches regarded as 'critical' or 'interpretive'. According to Blackmore and Lauder (2005) 'rationalist' approaches to policy analysis dominated the field up until the 1970s and were largely based on the presumption that experts trained in proper analytical techniques can apply them systematically to inform policy production. Nancy Shulock (1999) suggests that such approaches involve the optimistic view of the positivist social sciences, that policy analysis based in rationality was capable of reaching objective conclusions in order to solve problems. Many accounts of the field describe the emergence of more 'critical' orientations from the early 1970s, as new sociologies of knowledge, the rise of critical social science and the development of feminist perspectives on research practices brought into question the purported value neutrality of rationalist approaches (Blackmore and Lauder 2005; Marston 2004). With this shift, policy analysts began interrogating policy as a vehicle for mobilising, entrenching or marginalising political interests. In the 1980s, Douglas Torgenson (1986) suggested there had been three distinct 'phases' in the field, distinguished by the nature of the relationship between knowledge and politics: from positivism, where knowledge purports to replace politics (or values); to the critique of positivism, where politics purports to replace knowledge; to post-positivism, where, in his view, knowledge and politics attain a measure of reconciliation.

In *Women, Policy and Politics* the field was narrated in a different way. Of central focus was the way rationalist *and* post-positivist approaches in policy studies understand and work with 'social problems'. Looking across a spectrum of approaches to policy, Bacchi organised the field by '*the way in which different authors deal with policy problems*' (1999: 19, italics in original), bringing some of the theoretical developments in the sociology of social problems, post-structuralism, and variants of post-modernism to bear on policy studies. In Bacchi's account, approaches to policy were regarded in terms of the ontological status given to 'problems', that is, as either existing in 'reality' or as 'representations'. For example, some approaches treat problems as objective entities, 'out there', waiting to be solved. In contrast, approaches that treat problems as representations understand them as constructed: constituted through interpretive practices through which 'things take on meaning and value' (Shapiro 1988: xi, cited by Bacchi 2009a: 31). In *Women, Policy and Politics* the key difference in distinguishing understandings of policy did not hinge on whether policy making practice was seen as being primarily rational or primarily political (the distinction conventionally drawn) but instead focused on how policy *problems* were themselves understood in different accounts of policy making. Unpicking and re-stitching the field in this way produced an alternative schema for categorising approaches to policy, distinguished by those that focus on 'problem solution' and those concerned with 'problem representation' (Bacchi 1999: 21). This work highlighted the potential of policy analysis as a means of apprehending how meaning is created in and through policy processes. Thus Bacchi underlined the significance of knowledge practices and provided an impetus (and a framework) for the development of a reflexive policy studies.

The idea that social problems are socially constructed provides a direct challenge to realist presumptions in policy studies. The suggestion that 'social problems' are brought into being, rather than simply existing, waiting to be solved, corrected or addressed by government can be unsettling for those who spend a good deal of their time attempting to have situations regarded as oppressive, intolerable, or simply untenable 'addressed'. From the constructionist perspective, however, abiding situations become social problems through shifts in understandings. To make this idea thinkable, social constructionists have provided examples of issues that have come to be regarded as 'social problems' historically. In Australia, for example, domestic violence, 'hate crimes', homosexuality, and smoking have all been shown to have moved, over time, from the realm of the personal or private, to become issues regarded as requiring public attention or intervention. Similarly, comparative examples have been used to demonstrate the cultural specificity of social problems: teenage pregnancy, for example, is only a 'problem' in particular cultural contexts. Yet even when issues become politicised in this way, competing interpretations prevail. Interpretations will differ, for example, on the nature and scope of the 'problem', its causes and effects, and appropriate 'solutions'. The relatively recent identification of 'childhood obesity' as a social problem in rich democracies illustrates these processes well. Here, the previously personal issue of children's weight has come to be understood as a social problem requiring public interventions. The activities of a wide range of stakeholders, from health professionals to industry lobbies, have been important in the presentation of children's weight as a social problem. There are vast differences in the way the nature of this 'problem' is defined and diversity in the range of 'solutions' that have been proposed (Fawcett et al. 2010: 26). Rather than childhood obesity appearing on the landscape as a new phenomenon, or a newly 'discovered' one, it can be argued that children's weight has been newly represented as a 'problem'. As Bacchi explains '(t)his is what is meant by the sometimes misunderstood phrase that people do not discover problems, they create them' (Bacchi 1999: 9).

For many in the field, focussing on problem construction in policy heralds exciting possibilities. In 'problem solution' approaches, the focus on 'finding facts', 'solving problems' and 'making decisions' has encouraged the development of quite technical descriptions of policy processes, replete with models, maps and flowcharts. 'Cycles' feature heavily. Yet dominant depictions of policy processes as rational, balanced, objective, and orderly, undertaken in the main by people with considerable expertise and authority, are far from universally accepted. Numerous commentators have pointed out that the contested and ambiguous nature of policy making renders these portraits improbable (Colebatch 2000; 2007; Hancock 2006; Newman 2002; Yeatman 1998). The conventional focus on the instrumental dimensions of policy has, however, drawn policy analysts away from thinking about the more deep-seated aspects of policy processes, particularly the ways that policy shapes people's understanding of, and experience of, the world. Hal Colebatch (2007), for example, argues that policy processes are better understood in terms of the framing and reframing of problems. Switching focus from problem solution to problem representation enables governance to be conceptualised as more than a technocratic exercise.

Attention to competing interpretations in policy has a longer history than *Women, Politics and Policy*. Indeed, Colebatch's suggestion that policy involves the 'framing' and 'reframing' of problems is situated within a tradition of 'interpretive policy analysis' which has focussed on the values and beliefs expressed in a given policy, and on the processes by which these are communicated to and 'read' by various audiences (Yanow 2000; Colebatch 2006). Ginadomenico Majone (1989) argued that policy was essentially about argumentation: finding good reasons for doing things. This called for attention to the way in which ideas and observations are assembled into a meaningful and persuasive pattern, a process that Martin Rein and Donald Schon (1994) called 'framing'. But as Bacchi points out (1999: 39), there is a distinction to be made between a focus on *values* in policy and a concern with the production of meaning. It is here that her description of policy as discourse has been fundamental in the recasting of policy studies.

Apprehending policy as discourse shifts the focus to the role of policy in 'making' social problems in a very specific way. While there are various strands within the turn to discourse in policy studies, most draw, to some extent, on Michel Foucault's work, where the term discourse is used to make apparent the connection between knowledge practices and power relations (Bacchi 2009a; Goodwin 2011). In *Women, Policy and Politics* Bacchi began a detailed discussion of the 'nuts and bolts' involved in taking on Foucault's definition(s) of discourse and describing policy as discourse. I suggest 'began a detailed discussion', because, while the book addresses a raft of questions emerging from this conceptual shift, such as the distinction between language and discourse, the sources and effects of discourses, and the relationship between agency, intentionality and discourse, Bacchi continued (and continues) to develop her analysis of policy as discourse in later works (see Bacchi 2000; 2005; 2008; 2009a). In brief, describing policy as discourse involves starting from the assumption that all actions, objects and practices are socially meaningful and that the interpretation of meanings is shaped by the social and political struggles in specific socio-historical contexts. Thus, policy must be recognised as a cultural product: it is context specific. More than this, policy is involved in constituting culture by making meaning: as well as making problems and solutions, policy discourses make 'facts' and make 'truths'. Policy discourses are thus practices that have effects which include the constitution of subjects and subjectivities; the imposition of limitations on what can be said and what can be thought; as well as the 'lived' effects, or the material effects on people's lives (1999: 45). In scoping out a policy as discourse analysis approach, Bacchi reframed the very objects of policy studies: from problems to problematisations; from finding facts to the nature of facts; or from 'what works' to 'the working of things' (Shaw 2010).

Women, Policy and Politics also proposed an approach for interrogating problem representations. The approach, described as the '*What's the Problem Represented to be?*' approach, involves probing the conceptual underpinnings of problematisations—the assumptions and presuppositions, considering what is left unproblematised and ascertaining the effects of representations. Bacchi (1999: 12; 2009) suggests asking questions of policies and policy proposals about how subjects are constituted; what is likely to change; what is likely to stay the same and who is likely to benefit from specific representations. As such, she has also provided the field with a method—a contribution I return to in the final section of this chapter. Here I reiterate the significance of Bacchi's approach for the recasting of policy studies: indeed some accounts of 'the field' now refer to a new phase in policy studies that has been stimulated by her perspectives on policy, policy making and policy analysis. In Ruth Lister's book *Understanding Theory and Concepts in Social Policy* (2010), a full chapter dedicated to social constructionist approaches to policy is titled 'What's the problem?' Lister (2010: 152) explains: '(o)ne of the most fully worked accounts of social constructionism in social policy can be found in Carol Bacchi's *Women, Policy and Politics* (1999)'.

Developing a reflexive policy studies

The '*What's the Problem Represented to be?*' approach has been taken up in feminist policy analyses in two ways. One way has been to shed new light on the assumptions embedded in gender policies and in social policies defined more broadly. For example, feminist policy analysts have been keen to examine how dominant or marginal representations of gender and gender inequality appear in key policy documents and programs. This has involved asking if gender inequality features in policies and if so, in what way, and to what extent. In a sense, this work has drawn attention to the inclusion or exclusion of feminist visions, without necessarily unpacking the visions themselves. In contrast, work such as Elin Krivst and Elin Petersen's (2010) analysis of state constructions of 'paid domestic work' in Sweden and Spain demonstrates that Bacchi's approach is also useful for accessing the underlying normative and exclusionary assumptions in visions of gender equality. Their study of policy involves asking questions such as: 'which women (and men) are the *subject* of gender equality, which *visions* of gender equality are dominant and who is *excluded* or *marginalised* in this representation of the problem of gender inequality?' (Krivst and Petersen 2010: 186, emphasis in original).

Women, Policy and Politics encouraged feminists to turn their gaze to the problem representations which lodge in their own policy proposals and sharpened feminist awareness of how all policy proposals contain in-built assumptions, presuppositions, and biases, even their own. Flowing from this is the possibility that the gender equality policies feminists propose can be limiting as well as enabling. In the 1999 book, the '*What's the Problem Represented to be?*' approach was demonstrated through a reading of a range of issues commonly tied to the 'problem' of 'women's inequality', including the issues of pay equity, discrimination, access to education, child care, abortion and sexual harassment. While providing a guide to the '*What's the Problem Represented to be?*' approach, these examples also highlighted some of the normative visions contained within feminist policy proposals that might be problematic, or at least worthy of questioning. For example, Bacchi suggests that a normative vision in pay equity policy, equal opportunity and affirmative action legislation, policies promoting equality in education and policies relating to childcare hinges on an assumption that 'all women (and men) require to be free is some form of paid labour'. This vision, she argues, 'ignores the exploitation of many working people, and the importance of people's non-working lives' (1999: 202).

In a later work on the need for 'reflexive framing', Bacchi (2009b) points out that reflexivity has a number of meanings, and clarifies her usage of a Foucauldian conceptualisation of reflexivity. She explains: 'For Foucault reflexivity refers to the need to put in question our categories of analysis. In fact for Foucault reflexivity requires a *conscious* interrogation of taken-for-granted presuppositions and beliefs' (Bacchi, 2009b: 27, emphasis in original). In *Women, Policy and Politics,* Bacchi proposed, and illustrated, the significance of reflexive feminist policy analyses. In this way, she has impelled feminist researchers to put into question their own 'categories of analysis', and to consciously interrogate their own 'taken-for-granted presuppositions and beliefs'. This has been an important intervention in both feminist theory and politics, where the contours of a post-structuralist feminism continue to be mapped out and debated. Of particular concern for post-structuralist feminism has been the possibility of a feminist project (or projects) for social change when knowledge is conceptualised as contextually specific and contingent. Bacchi's approach to feminist policy studies works on this dilemma. Indeed, the insights which arose from analysing how 'women's inequality' had been problematised led her to propose a 'dual-focus' agenda to 'identify both ways in which interpretive and conceptual schemas delimit understandings, and the politics involved in the intentional deployment of concepts and categories to achieve political goals' (2005: 207).

As more examples of reflexive policy analyses emerge, it is becoming clear that Bacchi's approach enables policy researchers to not only uncover the normative nature of statements that appear to be obvious, inevitable or natural, and to test judgements about truth claims, but also to consider or imagine alternative ways of developing policy and practice. An example from my own work illustrates the potential of focusing on problem representations, but also the difficulties involved in disrupting dominant representations of policy problems. As part of the Gender Equity and Public Institutions (GEPI) project (see Schofield and Goodwin 2006; Connell 2007), I applied a '*What's the Problem Represented to be?*' approach in the analysis of the policy statements, policy documents and public reports on employment equality measures in the NSW public sector that had been produced between 1975 and 2002. These texts had been produced, in the main, by 'femocrats', policy officers located in the public sector agencies that had been established to promote women's equality. I found that the 'problem' was consistently represented in these texts as 'women's under-representation' in senior management positions, and that responsibility for the problem was largely attributed to women. In the spirit of exploring alternative policy approaches, the analysis suggested it was just as possible to conceptualise the 'problem' as men's *over-representation* in senior management: in 2002, around 80 per cent of senior managers were men, yet men constituted less than half of the total public sector workforce. If overrepresentation were seen as 'the problem', the measures taken would be significantly different. Instead of programs aimed at getting women into senior management, interventions would focus on reducing men's dominance at senior levels. Imagined alternatives include measures that would assist men to take on family roles (in order to de-gender divisions of responsibility around work/family), or that would re-frame different types of work as 'men's work' (such as part-time work, or ancillary work, or care-giving work).

Perhaps unsurprisingly, these proposals were rejected. Indeed, the response suggested that it would be untenable in the existing gender regime to represent the problem in such a way. That is, in the context of masculine dominance, it was important, for both feminists and others, that inequality in employment continue to be constituted as a 'women's problem'. Observing similar limitations on feminist interventions through public policy in Sweden, feminist political economist Agneta Stark (2008) asks if 'Don't Disturb the Men' is actually a viable gender equality strategy. Thus the example underlines the ongoing importance of feminists not only engaging in reflexive policy analysis, but also in struggles over the power to *make discourse*. As Stephen Ball (1990; 2006) suggests, these struggles involve changing institutional practices, power relations and social positions.

However, there is another reason my 'revelations' about the gender equity policies of the NSW government do not appear in any of the outputs of the GEPI project. This is that I had not been clear about my method. Although the work involved making explicit the normative assumptions embedded in the texts, my failure to articulate *how* these had been accessed rendered the analysis vulnerable to charges of unsystematised speculation. Rather than rejecting such charges as ideologically-based, I would like to suggest that there *is* a tendency not to declare method in policy as discourse research, and indeed in social research that uses discourse analysis techniques more broadly. 'Declaring method' in discourse analysis approaches means more than simply referring to epistemological principles or citing a methodological heritage, but involves being explicit about the steps and strategies involved in obtaining knowledge outside the existing system of meaning. One explanation for the tendency not to declare method in policy as discourse research relates to an attempt to avoid what has been called 'the positivist trap' of essentialising and prescribing research methods (Graham 2006). Another explanation is that we are often so taken by the 'surprises' that emerge from our research (very often identified as the 'dominant discourse/s') that the painstaking work involved in the revelation of concepts, statements, subject positions, binaries and logics that make up discursive forms seems by the by. I suggest that consciously declaring these 'little revelations' needs to be a key component of reflexive policy analysis. To this end, Bacchi's contribution of a declarable framework for doing the work of analysing problematisations in policy, described below as 'a method', can be considered a way forward.

The '*WPR*' approach: Providing a method

Where *Women, Policy and Politics* provided a rationale for and illustrations of a problem representation approach, Bacchi's later book *Analysing Policy: What's the Problem Represented to be?* (2009) sets out a range of strategies analysts can employ to investigate knowledge practices in policy production. Here the applicability of the '*What's the Problem Represented to be?*' (or '*WPR*') approach is carefully demonstrated, and examples are provided to illustrate how researchers and practitioners can operationalise fairly abstract ideas in the concrete tasks of analysing policy proposals, policies and programs. Specifically, Bacchi posits a set of questions that can be asked of a given policy text or set of texts in order to probe the conceptual underpinnings of problem representations. The basic questions appear in *Women, Policy and Politics,* but the new book illustrates how to apply the questions systematically (see Chapter 2, this volume, for the full list of questions).

The first question involves identifying the implied problem representations in specific policies or policy proposals. How is the text or texts presenting the problem to be addressed? The second question relates to the assumptions or presuppositions that underlie the representation of the problem. This process is distinct from identifying (or surmising) the assumptions or beliefs held by policy makers. Rather, the objective is to access the presumptions and presuppositions that lodge within problem representations. While a policy maker may 'believe' in a certain approach or course of action—for example, that small government or gender equality is desirable—these 'beliefs' will not necessarily lodge within the problem representation. Importantly, the approach is not concerned with the *intentional* shaping of issues, or with intentionality: indeed attempts to acquire knowledge about 'what policy makers *really* meant to do' runs counter to a concern with problem representations. Ascertaining these logics involves an exercise in Foucauldian archaeology and engaging in a form of discourse analysis: identifying key concepts and categories, and interrogating the binaries operating in policy.

The third question entails moving beyond the text or texts to explore how a particular representation of the problem has come about. Here the policy analyst is interested in how key concepts in the text/s have become legitimate, for example how the binaries employed have come to 'make sense' and the place of important categories in broader schemas of categorisation. It is suggested that Foucault's genealogical strategies are useful here. As Bacchi explains,

> [t]racing the 'history' of a current problem representation has a destabilising effect on problem representations that are often taken for granted. It also provides insights into the power relations that affect the success of some problem representation and the defeat of others. (Bacchi 2009a: 11)

The purpose of the fourth question, concerned with what has been left unproblematic in the problem representation, is to raise for reflection and consideration issues and perspectives that are silenced in identified problem representations. Drawing on cross-cultural or historical comparisons can render visible the way in which certain problem representations reflect specific institutional and cultural contexts and also provide examples of alternative representations. The fifth question moves the analyst to a concern with the effects of problem representations. These include symbolic and material effects: *discursive* effects which follow from the limits of what can be thought or said; *subjectification* effects which define who we are, how we feel about ourselves and who is attributed responsibility for a 'problem', as well as *lived* effects, such as the material impact of problem representations which can, for example, limit or enable access to resources, or cause or relieve emotional or material distress. The final question involves exploring how and where this representation of the problem has been produced, disseminated and defended. The aim of this question is to ascertain the means by which some problem representations become dominant, as well as the means by which dominant representations could be questioned, disputed and disrupted.

There is now a growing body of work that draws on empirical studies deploying a '*WPR*' approach. These types of studies are being undertaken in policy areas as diverse as housing, education, climate change policy, reprogenetics, Indigenous policy and health policy. For the reasons described above, feminist policy researchers have been particularly taken with the '*WPR*' approach as a method for interrogating policies that impact on women and on gender inequalities. As such, the approach has been applied in investigations of domestic violence policy, gender equity policy, gender mainstreaming and women's employment. However, this work is situated in a policy world in which positivist research methods continue to dominate. Indeed, in recent decades the emergence of an 'evidence-based policy' movement has contended that positivist research is perhaps *the* most important input into the policy process, on the assumption that it establishes a rational foundation for policy development, analysis and review. This 'new face' of policy analysis involves conceiving policy in a very traditional way, as rational, orderly and capable of producing objective solutions to 'problems'. Once again, 'knowledge' is seen as uncontested, capable of being translated into policy under the rubric of 'what works'. Janet Newman (2001: 69) suggests that the drive for 'evidence based policy' is a form of politics itself. This is because what constitutes 'evidence' and what is regarded as the proper conduct of research are both produced through discursive contestations.

Bacchi (2009: 271) also acknowledges that the tendency to concentrate on 'problem-solving' rather than 'problem-questioning' remains dominant, and is hesitant about the likelihood that official discourses regarding policy method will shift. She asks:

> Is this shift from 'problem-*solving*' to 'problem-*questioning*' likely to occur in the current climate? Probably not. But at least it should be possible to put in question the contemporary near hegemony of a 'problem-solving' paradigm. A WPR approach to policy analysis encourages such interrogation. The suggestion is that asking 'what's the problem represented to be?' will leaven, if you will, or counter-balance the fashionable weight accorded 'evidence' (271-72, emphasis in original).

In my view, leavening the weight accorded to 'evidence' will be further enabled by '*WPR*' researchers being more explicit about their method, not as a way of claiming methodological superiority, but as a way of engaging in struggles in the politics of policy. Rather than seeing policy research as a tool for producing 'knowledge' about problems, it may be more useful to see policy research as a tool for political participation. At a more basic level, laying out the steps taken to arrive at new insights can be seen as a 'gift' to other researchers undertaking '*WPR*' analyses.

Conclusion

In this chapter I have outlined some of the key ways in which Bacchi's work has contributed to the field of policy studies. The particular contributions I have identified in this account—the recasting of the field to include a focus on problematisations, the introduction of an approach that promotes reflexive policy studies, and the outlining of a method for analysing policy as discourse—clearly overlap with one another. The three contributions are based in the epistemological assumption that knowledge is a human construction and therefore many competing constructions of policy 'problems' are possible. It is, however, possible to deconstruct or defamiliarise policies and policy proposals in order to obtain knowledge that is critically different from the existing system of meaning. This type of analytic strategy is particularly important in policy practice because different constructions of policy problems will have different effects: discursive effects *and* 'lived' or material effects.

I conclude with a note on my own 'representation' of Bacchi's work as it appears in this chapter. In this chapter, I have assembled a narrative about *Women, Policy and Politics* in quite a specific way. My account has been produced in order to highlight the significant 'effects' of these contributions on a disciplinary field of practice. Shaping the discussion in this way has enabled me to demonstrate not only how Bacchi's work departs from the conventional concerns and dominant approaches in policy studies, but also to highlight why the '*WPR*' approach, specifically understood as a method, assists policy researchers in their attempts to identify, disrupt and challenge dominant representations of policy problems (and 'solutions'). Yet the transformation of the field should be seen an important *consequence* of this work, rather than an *intent*. If intent is to be garnered from Bacchi's work on policy analysis, it is to contribute to contemporary politics, albeit through a focus on problem representations. The concluding sentence in *Women, Policy and Politics* provides an apt statement of purpose:

> My goal…is to produce more reflexive feminist analyses and to assist in the difficult task of designing context-sensitive proposals which minimize losses and maximise gains. (1999: 207)

References

Bacchi, C. (1999) *Women, Policy and Politics: The construction of policy problems*, London: Sage.

—— (2000) 'Policy as Discourse: What does it mean? Where does it get us?' *Discourse: Studies in the cultural politics of education*, 21 (1): 45-57.

—— (2005) 'Discourse, Discourse Everywhere: Subject "agency" in feminist discourse Methodology', *NORA - Nordic Journal of Feminist and Gender Research*, 13 (3): 198-209.

—— (2008) 'The Ethics of Problem Representation: Widening the scope of ethical debate', *Policy and Society*, 25 (2): 3-22.

—— (2009a) *Analysing Policy: What's the Problem Represented to be?* Frenchs Forest: Pearson.

—— (2009b) 'The Issue of Intentionality in Frame Theory: The need for reflexive framing' in E. Lombardo, P. Meier and M. Verloo (eds) *The Discursive Politics of Gender Equality: Stretching, bending and policymaking*, London: Routledge.

Ball, S. J. (1990) *Politics and Policymaking in Education: Explorations in policy sociology*, London: Routledge.

—— (2006) *Education Policy and Social Class: The selected works of Stephen J. Ball*, London: Routledge.

Blackmore, J. and H. Lauder (2005) 'Researching Policy' in B. Somekh and C. Lewin (eds) *Research Methods in the Social Sciences*, London: Sage, 97-104.

Colebatch, H. K. (2000) *Policy*, Buckingham: Open University Press.

—— (ed.) (2006) *Beyond the Policy Cycle: The policy process in Australia*, Sydney: Allen and Unwin.

—— (2007) *Doing Policy, Doing Analysis: Accounting for policy in Australia,* Department of Public Policy and Administration, University of Brunei Darassalum.

Connell, R. (2006) 'Glass Ceilings or Gendered Institutions? Mapping the gender regimes of public sector worksites'. *Public Administration Review*, 66 (6): 837-849.

Fawcett, B., S. Goodwin, G. Meagher and R. Phillips (2010) *Social Policy for Social Change.* Melbourne: Palgrave Macmillan.

Goodwin, S. (2011) 'Analysing Policy as Discourse: Methodological advances in policy analysis', L. Markauskaite, P. Freebody, and J. Irwin, Jude (eds), *Methodological Choices and Research Designs for Educational and Social Change: Linking scholarship, policy and practice*, New York: Springer.

Graham, L. (2005) 'Discourse Analysis and the Critical Use of Foucault', Australian Association for Research in Education 2005 Annual Conference, Sydney, 27th November-1st December. Available HTTP: <http://eprints.qut.edu.au/2689/1/2689.pdf> (accessed August 2009).

Krivst, E. and E. Petersen (2010) 'What has Gender Equality Got to do With it? An analysis of policy debates surrounding domestic services in the welfare state of Sweden and Spain' in *NORA - Nordic Journal of Feminist and Gender Research*, 18 (3): 185-203.

Lister, R. (2010) *Understanding Theories and Concepts in Social Policy*, Bristol: Policy Press.

Majone, G. (1989) *Evidence, Argument, and Persuasion in the Policy Process*. New Haven: Yale University Press.

Marston, G. (2004) *Social Policy and Discourse Analysis: Policy change in public housing*, Hampshire: Ashgate Publishing.

Newman, J. (2001) *Modernising Governance: New Labour, policy and society*, London: Sage.

Rein, M. and D. Schon (1994) *Frame Reflection: Toward the resolution of intractable policy controversies*, New York: Basic Books.

Schofield. T. and S. Goodwin (2006) 'Gender Politics and Public Policy Making: Prospects for advancing gender equality' in *Policy and Society: Journal of Public, Foreign and Global Policy*, 24 (4): 25-44.

Shaw, S. (2010) 'Reaching the Parts that Other Theories and Methods Can't Reach: How and why a policy-as-discourse approach can inform health-related policy', *Health*, 14 (2): 196-212.

Shulock, N. (1999) 'The Paradox of Policy Analysis: If it is not used, why do we produce so much of it?' in *Journal of Policy Analysis and Management*, 18 (2): 226-244.

Stark, A. (2008) 'Don't Disturb the Men: A viable gender-equality strategy?' in N. Kabeer and A. Stark (ed.) *Global Perspectives on Gender Equality: Reversing the Gaze*, Routledge: New York, 229-243.

Torgenson, D. (1986) 'Between Knowledge and Politics: Three faces of policy analysis' *Policy Sciences*, 19: 33-59.

Yanow, D. (2000) *Conducting Interpretive Policy Analysis*, London: Sage.

Yeatman, A. (1998) *Activism and the Policy Process*, Sydney: Allen and Unwin.

4 | Spaces between: Elaborating the theoretical underpinnings of the '*WPR*' approach and its significance for contemporary scholarship

ANGELIQUE BLETSAS

This chapter reflects upon Carol Bacchi's (1999; 2009) '*What's the Problem Represented to be?*' ('*WPR*') approach to policy analysis, commenting in particular on the wider theoretical underpinnings of the approach, and the influence that both had upon my doctoral thesis. The '*WPR*' approach takes an innovative and important theoretical orientation to policy studies and to critical analysis more generally. Of central concern in this chapter is the way that the '*WPR*' approach side-steps, avoids, and challenges taken-for-granted approaches to 'problem solving' as well as its rejection of the idea that problems exist 'out there' to be stumbled upon. It is in the context of these analytical moves, elaborated below, that the '*WPR*' approach insists that modes of acting are contingent upon ways of knowing and that, connectedly, to reflect critically upon a subject *is* a political act. Considering understandings of knowledge, critical analysis and scholarship more widely, the chapter also addresses the ways in which the critical impulse central to Bacchi's scholarship sits in a tense relationship with orthodox understandings of scholarship.

This last point recalls the title of the chapter, 'Spaces between'. I aim to deploy the metaphor of space to imply a variety of meanings. Space can be understood as distance, and as a metaphor can signal conflicts and contrasts in the ways we understand the world, competing meanings and distinct world-views. The metaphor of space as distance—and connectedly the challenge of distances to be travelled—thus raises the question of how we find our way from one viewpoint to another, and the further question of whether all conceptual distances can be traversed. Are there spaces—conceptual distances and differences—that cannot be reconciled, sites over which there is no meeting point? Should it be regarded a bad thing if this is so? Where I discuss the space between the understanding of critical scholarship practice developed in Bacchi's work and that prevalent in orthodox understandings of scholarship I suggest that perhaps this constitutes an instance of insurmountable conceptual distance.

It may be seen then that, as a metaphor, the notion of 'space' can reflect conceptual conflicts and the incommensurability, or rather, the radical distinctness, of points of view. These are ideas which, as I will shortly address, are central to post-structuralist thought which underlies Bacchi's work. Yet, while the metaphor of space can signal distance, it can also signal new possibilities—a facilitating function, creating not a void of incommensurability but an area of movement and extension. To 'give space' or 'create space' is metaphorically to excavate an area which it is possible to occupy, to move within, that was not previously available. This is the first meaning I wish to draw out from the metaphor of space. The chapter begins with an account of one of the key intellectual contributions of Bacchi's '*WPR*' approach, which is that it creates a space, an intellectual terrain, wherein it becomes possible to pause and critically reflect on the taken-for-granted nature of problem-solving.

The '*WPR*' approach as post-structuralist method: Space in which to think

The '*What's the Problem Represented to be?*' approach can be described as a particular methodology for the study of policy (and other areas of thought/analysis/action), which rests on two central propositions. The first proposition is that, rather than evaluate policies for their ability to 'solve' problems, we need to study the way policies *construct* problems (Bacchi 2009: ix-xvii). On this point the '*WPR*' approach claims that it is possible to read backwards from any policy proposal—that is, from the solution offered—just what the 'problem' is understood—*represented*—to be (Bacchi 2009: x-xi). The second key proposition is that problematisations are central to the practice of government—to *governing* (Bacchi 2009: ix-xiii). I elaborate both points throughout the chapter. As a methodology the '*WPR*' approach goes on to provide six guiding questions which enable analysis at this level of investigating the construction of policy problems[1] (Bacchi 2009: 2). As the focus of the chapter is to elaborate the theoretical precepts of the '*WPR*' approach and its understanding of 'problems' and problematisations, I will not be applying the '*WPR*' approach in methodological form. Instead, I am concerned to show *how* the '*WPR*' approach creates this space in which it becomes possible to think 'problems' in a distinct and different way from that ordinarily available in policy studies and political analysis more generally.

As noted, the '*WPR*' approach insists that problem representations matter practically and politically. In itself, this is not a particularly controversial claim. Much political debate can be seen to occur over, or even as, attempts to fix representations of problems in one way or another. A relevant example here may be identified in debates on poverty and welfare, the policy area with which my doctoral thesis is concerned, to be discussed later in the chapter. There is a long history of political debate over the cause of poverty as a social problem. Is it *structurally* caused—the result of economic policies such as the casualisation of the labour market, and/or the product of systemic discrimination against particular groups in society?

---

[1] It is important to note that though the focus in this chapter is on the construction of poverty in particular policies and other texts, the '*WPR*' approach does not merely advocate textual analysis and is applicable to other sites.

Or is poverty the result of lack of thrift, bad choices, and other personal, that is, *individual* failings? This debate is a debate over how the problem of poverty *ought to be* understood. In other words, it is a debate over what kind of a problem poverty is *represented* to be. As a debate, this argument over the causes of poverty usually takes the form of a structure/agency debate. If one wishes to engage the poverty debate one generally does so by taking one side or the other of this structure/agency debate.[2]

Applying the '*WPR*' approach to the poverty debate has two immediate effects. Firstly, it enables an analysis which shows that, in different policy proposals, what is problematic about poverty, i.e. the 'problem', is represented differently. If, for example, one were to apply the '*WPR*' approach to a policy proposal, such as the Australian federal government's current policy of Compulsory Income Management for individuals on welfare, one could demonstrate that, quite clearly, it is inappropriate use of income which in this policy is represented to be the 'problem'. Compulsory Income Management redirects half of the income paid to individuals who live in selected—generally Indigenous—communities, and who are in receipt of welfare, to be paid as credit on a card that may only be used in select grocery and clothing stores. In this way the policy specifically and intentionally restricts the use of a portion of welfare income so that it is necessarily spent on fundamentals such as food and clothing. From this cursory analysis it can be said that, implicitly, the policy of Compulsory Income Management takes an individualistic approach to the 'problem' of poverty: the policy is directed at affecting the behaviour of *individuals* in a didactic manner, instructing them on the 'proper' use of income.

In contrast, if one were to apply the '*WPR*' approach to policy suggestions to increase levels of welfare income, suggestions which are frequently endorsed by third sector organisations (for example see Karvelas 2010; Gordon 2010) but which tend not to translate to actual government legislation, it would be possible to show that the problem is constructed in this instance as inadequate income, in contrast to inappropriate use of a limited income. This policy suggestion understands the problem of poverty in more of a 'structuralist' mode. What individuals require, on this account, is not instruction in how to manage their income, but a greater income than what they receive currently.

While applying a '*WPR*' approach facilitates analysis at this relatively non-controversial level of identifying competing problem representations, the contention that we are ruled through problematisations (Bacchi 2009: xiii), the second key proposition of the '*WPR*' approach, involves a further move. This additional move puts in question the idea that 'poverty' has an independent existence as a 'problem' to be solved by (state) government and other experts. The primary effect of this analytic move is to lead us to ask quite different questions to those ordinarily raised in debates over poverty and its representation as a particular kind of problem. Importantly, to make this claim—that poverty does not have an independent existence as a 'problem'—does not amount to putting in question the *reality* of poverty—

---

2   Alice O'Connor (2001: 3-18) discusses the way that the structure/agency debate has come to serve as a fault-line in US debates about poverty and welfare. Though her theoretical approach is in key ways different from that taken in this chapter, her analysis is in many ways commensurate with the argument developed here.

understood as the experience of extreme disadvantage and deprivation. Nor does it somehow imply that the existence of poverty is 'ok' or acceptable—that it is not *problematic*. This stance should not be taken to imply either an empirical position or a normative position. Instead this analytic move calls into question the *relationship* between poverty and government policy. It argues that this relationship is not necessary or natural but a product of a particular way of both thinking about poverty *and* thinking and enacting the practice of governing. This critical approach addresses poverty as a *problematisation*.

As has been intimated above, in the '*WPR*' approach 'problems' are not treated as if they exist as discrete and independent entities out in the social world for experts and analysts to come upon and resolve. Instead, it is argued that, in the present context, rule—the practice of governing—occurs through problematisations (Bacchi 2009: xiii). This is to claim, in other words, that the 'problem-solving' in which policies are involved is specific to a particular style of governing. Importantly in this analysis 'governing' is understood as a verb—the practice of organising and administering society. As Foucault (1991: 93) famously put it in his essay on the historic emergence of a *govern*-mentality, government, as a style of rule, concerns the 'right disposition of things'. To analyse poverty as a *problematisation* is therefore to ask questions about how the government of poverty sits in relation to the wider configuration of governing practices. It is not to claim that poverty is merely the product of ways of seeing the world.

Given this understanding of government, as occurring through particular problematisations, applying the '*WPR*' approach to an analysis of poverty facilitates a space in which it is possible to side-step the structure/agency debate about the causes of poverty in order to ask a separate set of equally political questions, such as: *how* did poverty come to be seen as a 'problem' for governments and other experts to address?[3] Why is it poverty, and not some related issue—inequality, wealth *etc.*—that has come to be seen as the 'problem'? What forms of governing practice (surveillance, discipline, self-government, *etc.*) are enabled where poverty is constructed in this way as a problem? What are the effects of this formation—including, and in particular, the lived effects for those who are poor? These are examples of the kinds of questions that the '*WPR*' approach directs us to ask. In my view, that this is so is one of the benefits of putting into question the taken-for-granted nature of problem solving, for, as long as we are stuck on the intractable debate, in this instance, of how to represent the 'problem' of poverty, we fail to recognise that the relationship between poverty and government is not neutral, natural or apolitical.

I wish again to emphasise that this is not a normative position but an *analytic* one. There is no implication that poverty *should not be* an object of government policy. Rather, there is a sceptical stance as regards how and why this has come to be so. To question the independent nature of 'problems' is not quite the same thing as claiming that all is right with the world and that political interventions are not required. Instead, and as I have been arguing, to question

---

[3] As a point of note, it is worth clarifying that this historic question on the relationship between poverty and contemporary modes of governing is not one I directly address in my thesis. This historic question has already been addressed by Mitchell Dean (1991) in his detailed, informative, and instructive book, *The Constitution of Poverty: towards a genealogy of liberal governance.*

the way problems are understood in particular policies is rather to question what their relation to current forms of government is. As Bacchi sets out in the introduction to her 2009 book:

> In asking how governing takes place the aim is to understand how order is maintained, and how we live within and abide by rules. The concern with public policy, therefore, includes but extends beyond laws and legislation to encompass 'a general understanding of societal administration' (Dean and Hindess 1998: 17). Laws or legislation are taken as starting points for asking questions about how governing (governance) in a broad sense occurs on a daily basis. Of particular interest are the roles of experts and professionals in this process. (Bacchi 2009: ix)

The interest then, is with the effects of power, with power effects. Importantly, what the concern with power effects signals, is that it is not just the question of how problems are *spoken* of that is at stake in the analysis of problematisations. Rather, such analysis is primarily concerned with the outcomes and material implications that arise when phenomena are constituted in particular ways as particular kinds of 'problems' (Bacchi 1999: 2).

Another way of clarifying the position that the '*WPR*' approach takes on understanding and analysing problems is available in an argument by Robert Chia (1996). Chia (1996: 32-33) succinctly captures the critical outlook at the core of post-structuralist modes of analysis such as the '*WPR*' approach where he argues that it is not the existence of objects that is challenged by post-structuralism—but the existence of objects as *fixed*.[4] The important distinction in understanding post-structuralism is not between the real and the imagined, between being and nothingness, but as Chia (1996: 32-33) formulates, between being and *becoming*. Chia (1996: 36-38) posits that what post-structuralism involves is a substitution of the ontology of being—the idea of social phenomena as fixed and concrete—which he claims is a taken-for-granted starting point in most academic scholarship, with an ontology of becoming. This idea is well established in the '*WPR*' approach where it is argued that what needs to be studied in the analysis of policy is not, to continue the example, poverty *as it exists as a problem*, but rather, poverty as it has *come to be constituted* as one.

From this analysis it is clear that the conceptualisation central to the '*WPR*' approach—that 'problems', social phenomena, do not have an independent existence—does not lead to the view that these phenomena do not exist *per se*, or that they *only* exist in the theories we have about them. The conceptualisation of problems in the '*WPR*' approach may be more accurately articulated as the claim that, as phenomena, 'problems' are always and endlessly being actively constituted; they are therefore never finished or fixed. If 'problems' are not fixed and never finished then what this requires is that, rather than try to 'represent' them *as they really are*, our analysis shift to investigating the ways in which these phenomena are *actively constituted* (Chia 1996: 33, 37). It is precisely this style of analysis which the '*WPR*' approach advocates.

Above I outlined the ways in which, by focusing on social phenomena—policy 'problems'—not as fixed but in terms of the way they are actively constituted, Bacchi's

---

[4] Chia actually uses the term 'postmodernism' and not 'post-structuralism' in his article. However, for the purpose of the current discussion the two terms are interchangeable.

'*What's the Problem Represented to be?*' approach creates a space in which it is possible to side-step the usual debates about the specific ways poverty is *represented* in order to ask a different set of questions about poverty (and by extension any other social phenomena) and the practice of governing. As a consequence of this critical process the '*WPR*' approach politicises the conceptual apparatuses through which we ordinarily 'problem solve'. In doing so Bacchi's '*WPR*' approach opens up a space from within which it becomes possible to intervene critically in these problem-solving conceptual apparatuses. For, as I now turn to consider, post-structuralist analytics, in arguing that we ought to study phenomena in their states of becoming, challenge not only established ontologies but also established ways of understanding scholarship.

The '*WPR*' approach as an analytics: Reflecting on scholarship practice

There are many ways in which scholarship and analysis have been understood and, as I do not mean to generalise, for my purpose here I will keep to my example of poverty as an area of research and analysis. Historically poverty research has operated as an empirical science. It is taken for granted that there is a phenomenon termed 'poverty', or relatedly, 'deprivation', 'disadvantage', and 'experts'—usually economists and social scientists[5]—go into the field to extract data which they then analyse and with which they hope to inform policy makers so that they may act and respond in an informed and rational manner.

The understanding of scholarship implicit in empirical poverty research, as I have described it here, fits within a 'rational' understanding of policy making and resonates with the current focus on 'evidence-based' policy approaches. As Bacchi (2009: 240-55) discusses in her 2009 book, in contrast to the '*WPR*' approach, rational and evidence-based policy approaches are approaches to knowledge and its role in the formation of policy that are predicated on the idea of social problems as fixed entities and scientific research as neutral and impartial. Their advocates assert that policy should be informed by this neutral research which will tell us what the 'evidence' is as to 'what works' on any given subject (see for example The Coalition for Evidence-Based Policy 2011). Established poverty research, along with 'evidence-based' approaches to policy making, thus presupposes that a space exists between experts and analysts who study poverty and poverty in its concreteness. Indeed, if we look at the history of poverty research, early pioneers of 'modern' poverty research practice such as Seebohm Rowntree in the UK and Ronald Henderson in Australia specifically attempted to create a neutral 'scientific' approach to poverty analysis so that poverty research could be free of the moralistic, frequently punitive, discourse which has almost always attached to it (Travers & Richardson 1992: 31-32).

Much in contrast to rational and evidence-based approaches, the post-structuralist 'ontology of becoming', as Chia (1996: 32-33) terms it, challenges the distinction between the phenomena and the expert, arguing that the relationship between them is more complex

---

[5] Bessant et al. (2006: 154) note, for example, that a 1990 bibliographic survey by Diana Encel finds that, of all Australian research on wealth and income distribution, over 80 per cent is contributed by economists.

than frequently acknowledged. What such a claim amounts to is not as simple as suggesting that 'discourse' or 'talk' on a given subject has a direct and immediate effect on that subject. Rather, it signals a kind of embeddedness: a radical connection between our ways of knowing the world and our ways of occupying it—of 'being' in it. This point is sometimes taken to be controversial, and I elaborate what I mean by keeping to my example of the poverty debate.

As mentioned above, debate over the representations of poverty and its causes usually, indeed almost always, takes the form of a structure/agency debate. To claim that how we know poverty is complex is not to suggest that it is not possible to argue one side of this debate over the other. It may well be the case that one side might be more persuasive than the other and a variety of interesting and important criteria might be called upon to determine which side of the debate we 'ought' to take and why. I most certainly find one account more persuasive than the other. However, no debate had at this level is able to explain *why* it is that poverty has come to be treated as the subject of a debate between structural explanations and individualistic explanations. The structure/agency debate is not a product of something inherent to poverty—it is a product of western forms of sociological and philosophical thought. Thus, however many times we survey people who are poor, asking increasingly intrusive questions about their lifestyle and diet, no answer will be found as to *why* it is that at the present moment debates over the 'poverty knowledge' (O'Connor 2001) of experts take a form highly reminiscent of what Foucault (2003: 340-65) termed the 'empirico-transcendental doublet'. That answer is far more likely to be found by asking how these two terms, structure and agency, finitude and transcendence, have become central to western sociology. What the post-structuralist ontology highlights then, is that how we think about poverty is a product of *how we think* far more than it is a product of something enduring in the nature of poverty. There is nothing inherent to poverty which causes this contemporary debate or the particular structure/agency form it takes.

It is this insight, this level of inquiry that the '*WPR*' approach, with its wider post-structuralist premises, is concerned with. It creates a space from which it becomes possible to ask, quite simply, how have taken-for-granted 'problems'—whether they are policy problems or conceptual problems such as the structure/agency debate itself—come to be taken for granted? It is my view that these are questions worth asking, and so it was that, from within this conceptual space, in my doctoral thesis I eschewed engaging arguments which made definitive claims about poverty in order to instead study these claims about poverty for what they could be seen to reveal about trends in government. Having addressed the theoretical underpinnings of the '*WPR*' approach, why I consider them to be so important, and how they came to inform the general direction of my doctoral thesis, below I outline a brief overview of the actual argument developed in the thesis.

Poverty and the emergent governmentality of affluence

The starting problematic of my doctoral thesis, which I began in 2005, lay in the observation that, increasingly, poverty in countries such as Australia was being represented as a problem which had by and large been solved. In media accounts and popular discourse only 'residual' issues such as 'welfare dependence' were (and are) considered to linger, along with pockets of disadvantage, or what empirical poverty researchers term 'geographic poverty'. This narrow conception of deprivation and disadvantage reflects the limited extent to which poverty was publicly and politically acknowledged, a situation which continues today. In so far as poverty was being constructed in this way, as by and large solved, 'residual' poverty was in turn constructed in individualistic, frequently behavioural, terms.

A prime example of the move towards an individualistic account of poverty as a 'residual problem' can be identified in the work of commentators such as David McKnight (2005: 12-13) and Clive Hamilton (2006: 21, 29-31)—names which are generally associated with the political left, where structuralist accounts of poverty have traditionally been advanced. Hamilton in particular is a notable figure in this regard as he had argued against groups such as the Centre for Independent Studies (CIS) who put forward the case that today 'poverty' is primarily behavioural (see for example Sullivan 2000; for counter-argument see Hamilton 2005). Yet by 2006 Hamilton was himself claiming that:

> Not only are those remaining in poverty, or significant material hardship, a small minority of the population, it is also no longer tenable to argue their deprivation is an inherent part of the economic system. In his book *Beyond Left and Right*, David McKnight reminds us that poverty is generated at the level of the family and is associated with family breakdown, substance abuse, mental illness and poor education. (Hamilton 2006: 21)

In the 2006 essay quoted above, Hamilton (2006: 21) goes on to clarify that he is not suggesting that the capitalist system is perfect or that all of the problems of inequality and injustice have been 'solved' in their entirety. Nonetheless, as described above, the problem of poverty is, for Hamilton (2006: 21), primarily a residual problem of marginal groups at the outskirts of mainstream society.

Unlike Hamilton, I find dubious this understanding of poverty as a 'residual' problem. Of particular concern is the way that the representation of poverty as a residual problem can be seen to be connected to punitive policy solutions. A prime example of the kinds of punitive interventions to which this understanding of poverty as a 'residual' problem can be seen to be connected is Compulsory Income Management, also known as 'Welfare Quarantining', mentioned earlier in the chapter. Compulsory Income Management first began as policy in Australia in 2007, as part of the then-Howard Government's *Northern Territory Emergency Response Act 2007* (NTER), the 'intervention' into select Indigenous communities of the Northern Territory. Among other measures, the NTER involved the suspension of the *Racial Discrimination Act 1975* (Cth) in the Northern Territory so that Compulsory Income Management could be implemented and half of the welfare income paid fortnightly to recipients living in these communities would now be paid as credit on a card which could be used only at select grocery and clothing stores and, in some instances, on rent. As described above, this policy reveals an individualistic understanding of poverty: it directs itself at altering the behaviour of individuals and the way they spend their income, not at the wider context in which such 'individual' decisions are made.

The given rationale behind the NTER and the introduction of Compulsory Income Management through the card system was that this was a way of preventing abuse of children which had been documented as a significant issue in Wild and Anderson's (2007) 'Ampe Akelyernemane Meke Mekarle: Little Children are Sacred' Report (Hinkson 2007: 1). Wild and Anderson were specifically mandated to report on incidence and issues concerning sexual abuse of Aboriginal children in the Northern Territory (2007: 4). In their Report they called for a radical and urgent new approach to the social issues facing communities of the Northern Territory, issues which, they asserted, had long been acknowledged (Wild and Anderson 2007: 5-7). One of the recommendations made in the Report is that the Commonwealth Government investigate the re-introduction of food vouchers in lieu of cash income for individuals on welfare (Wild and Anderson 2007: 171). The rationale offered on this point in the Report is that such a move may be a positive way of addressing issues of alcoholism in Northern Territory communities (Wild and Anderson 2007: 171).

There is a confluence of issues that often goes unremarked in discussions of the merits of Compulsory Income Management policy. While it is beyond the scope of this chapter to address them in detail it is important to state clearly what these too frequently conflated issues are. Residents of the Northern Territory communities affected by the NTER who have publicly supported the implementation of Compulsory Income Management usually make the point that having their income forcibly directed in this way means that they are in some measure freed of demands for money by other members of the community (for example see Hall 2010)—though others have also reported being concerned by the policy precisely for this reason (for example see Kearney 2007), and still others have claimed that the policy is failing to protect them from such harassment (for example see Hall 2010). This issue of harassing income from individuals is colloquially referred to as 'humbug' or 'humbugging': demanding cash or other resource assistance from relatives and community members. In reports on the subject it is frequently associated with issues of alcohol abuse (Ferguson 2008; Hall 2010). The issue of humbug constitutes a very separate scenario to that which suggests that individuals are failing to purchase necessary food items for their children because they are instead spending their income on alcohol for themselves—the meaning usually implied by the term 'welfare quarantining' (see Hinkson on Mal Brough 2007: 5).

It is misleading to conflate these two issues—the issue of abuse of children where it is produced by the neglect of substance-dependent care-providers, and the issue of individuals being harassed for their welfare income by substance-dependent and other relatives and community members and, as a consequence, being left short of money for necessities. In one scenario parents and caregivers are seen to wilfully neglect children in their care, in the other parents and care providers are *themselves* victims of harassment. Both sets of issues may well occur in the same communities, perhaps even in the same families, nonetheless they present different phenomena, ostensibly different 'problems' requiring different 'solutions'. There is no reason to believe that conflating the two issues is likely to be of assistance to either policy makers or children in need.

It is also important to recognise that, though it is the case that the rationale behind Compulsory Income Management was (at least initially) connected to the goal of preventing abuse of children, welfare recipients who were targeted for welfare quarantining did not have to have a history or even an allegation of child abuse against them. They simply had to be living in the targeted Indigenous communities of the Northern Territory and in receipt of welfare (Hinkson 2007: 3). It was for this reason that the *Racial Discrimination Act 1975* had to be suspended in order for the NTER, and the 'quarantining' of welfare income, to be implemented (Gibson 2010: 8). No rationale or justificatory logic has ever been forwarded outlining why such an approach, clearly encroaching upon the civil rights of individuals who had no connection to the abuse of children, was considered to contribute to improved outcomes for abused and neglected children.

Since 2007 and the introduction of the NTER we have had a change of federal government, a change some commentators, including state politicians, hoped would result in the 'roll-back' of at least some of the key tenets of the NTER (see for example Ravens 2007). Though there is widespread agreement that many Indigenous communities in the Northern Territory face complex and challenging issues there is little agreement that the NTER presents an appropriate or effective solution and it has attracted significant critical attention (see for example the edited collection of essays by Altman and Hinkson 2007; Gibson 2010). Significantly, in 2009 UN Special Rapporteur James Anaya found the NTER to put Australia in breach of its commitment to upholding both the International Convention on the Elimination of All Forms of Racial Discrimination and the International Covenant on Civil and Political Rights, treaties to which Australia is a signatory (Anaya 2009).

Despite such criticism the NTER has continued with only minor amendments. In November 2009 Federal Labor Minister Jenny Macklin announced that she would be reinstating the *Racial Discrimination Act 1975* in the Northern Territory but not repealing the policy of Compulsory Income Management (Macklin 2009; Lunn 2009). Instead, implementation of this policy was now to apply to any community of 'extreme disadvantage' anywhere in the country—whether Indigenous or non-Indigenous (Lunn 2009). Despite the widening of the ambit of Compulsory Income Management, the implications of this policy for Indigenous communities are still unique. I acknowledge and address this fact in my thesis and I describe the way the policy reiterates a disturbingly commonplace understanding of Aboriginal peoples and Aboriginal culture as being developmentally inferior to 'post-materialist' 'western' culture (Bletsas 2010: 184-87). For the purpose of this chapter, however, my interest is with the way that the policy can be seen to represent poverty as something that is restricted to specific communities—that it is residual in this way, the product of internal dysfunction rather than a consequences of broad social relationships. What is more, the extension of welfare quarantining to communities, Indigenous or non-Indigenous, on the basis of their poverty demonstrates the extent to which the earlier association with child abuse, though still mobilised on occasion, has now been more or less dropped, and the policy of Compulsory Income Management is becoming instead a default way of treating individuals who are identified as belonging to a community of 'significant disadvantage', in Minister

Macklin's (2009) words. The trajectory of this policy thus exemplifies the logic that poverty today is residual—a problem of dysfunctional communities on the margin of the greater social whole who need to be made subject to didactic and intrusive forms of government so that they can be—not necessarily reformed in a moral sense—but advanced in a developmental sense: so they can be caught up to the rest of 'us', the affluent, western, mainstream.

What my thesis (Bletsas 2010) offers in relation to these developments—the representation of poverty as a residual problem and the increasingly intrusive policy measures which accompany it—is an articulation of the governmental logic, which I term a governmentality of affluence, upon which such policies are predicated. I trace out, from work such as Hamilton's (2006; 2003), McKnight's (2005) and their ideologically opposed counterparts at the CIS (for example Saunders 2003), the growing dominance of a developmental narrative which, since the 1960s, has increasingly constructed poverty as connected to an older and allegedly receding social world, counterposing the 'problems' of welfare and inequality with 'new' problems of post-materialism, individual aesthetics and self-actualisation.

I do not 'discover' this post-materialist discourse in my thesis, and it is not novel to suggest that a post-materialist discourse treats poverty as concerned with a basic (and base) material aspect of human being, and self-actualisation—however defined—with a higher aesthetic order. In fact it is a fairly straightforward summation of the post-materialist thesis (for example Inglehart 1977: 285-86, 363). Influenced by a post-structuralist thematic, I remain highly sceptical of the developmental narrative of a necessary and natural arc of universal human being that is central to post-materialism. I reject the idea of a 'natural' shift from the problems of poverty and scarcity to the problems of affluence and abundance. I do not treat these 'problems'—poverty, self-actualisation, *etc.*—as if they exist somewhere out there to be stumbled over by social theorists and political commentators. Instead I examine them in terms of their connection to a wider configuration of governmental practices. This is what I intend where I argue that this developmental narrative signifies the emergence of a governmental motif of affluence. From this position I contend that the understanding of poverty as residual is *not* a reflection of some *fact* that today the poor *really are* the dysfunctional, transgressive selves that they have always been held to be by those who equate financial poverty with individual lack, but that instead affluence has today emerged as a *problematisation* through which government is conceptualised and enacted. In so far as this is so, poverty becomes displaced—though not dispensed with—as a governmental motif.

The initial premise I began with is that the relationship between poverty and government was neither neutral nor natural. The argument that I make then is that the displacement of poverty as a governmental thematic is not simply a reflection of some change in the constitution of poverty, as commentators from Clive Hamilton (2006: 21, 29-31) to Peter Saunders (2003: 12-13) of the CIS suggest, but instead reflects a change in the construction of governing logics. In the lead up to the 2010 Australian election, Opposition Leader Tony Abbott told voters he wanted to lead them in a transformation from 'a welfare state to an opportunity society' (quoted in Needham 2010). This kind of statement highlights what is meant by a governmental motif of affluence and the way it displaces poverty. I consider it not just a new way of *talking* government but an emergent way of *thinking* and thus *enacting* the practice of government—an emergent way of claiming to know the 'right disposition of things' (Foucault 1991: 93).

There is a great deal more that could be said on the idea of an emergent motif of affluence and its implications for government. However the purpose of this chapter has not been to elaborate the thesis of a governmentality of affluence but rather to elaborate how Bacchi's *'What's the Problem Represented to be?'* approach, with its wider post-structuralist premises, creates the space in which it is possible to make this kind of argument. It accomplishes this by side-stepping the debate over the cause(s) of poverty—how the problem 'ought to be represented'—by challenging the notion that poverty is a fixed social phenomenon, and by examining instead the connections between ways of knowing poverty and ways of governing society. The space created is one in which knowledge claims such as those put forward by poverty research experts, as well as those put forward by commentators and critics such as Hamilton, McKnight and researchers at the Centre for Independent Studies, are not regarded as neutral accounts, or even as partisan accounts of a simple social reality, but instead are seen as *complex interventions into* social reality.

In refusing to treat research as simply neutral and descriptive, post-structuralism in general, and the *'WPR'* approach in particular, offer the possibility of research as a political engagement. On this account, to study a subject is to intervene in it. Furthermore, in taking such a stance, both the *'WPR'* approach and post-structuralist scholarship insist that certainty and finality of any 'knowledge' are forever out of reach—if phenomena are not fixed but endlessly in flux then there can be no 'final word' or definitive account of them. The suggestion that in turn arises from this conceptualisation of scholarship is that perhaps, then, certainty and finality are not the only goals towards which our analysis should strive. If knowledge of a subject is necessarily active and constitutive then, *as well as* evaluating scholarship for intellectual rigour and internal consistency, perhaps we need to evaluate it in terms of its political effects.

There are, of course, implications in conceptualising phenomena as in flux and knowledge as constitutive and political in this way. It is the case that post-structuralism and the *'WPR'* approach offer the possibility of conceptualising research as political engagement, but in doing so they insist that all of our intellectual, analytical and conceptual engagements are necessarily political. This can at times be frustrating, and is a difficult position to occupy comfortably. I certainly do not mean to deny that intellectual certainty is a desirable end state of analysis! Yet, this discomfort and frustration is itself important. For, while an uncomfortable analytical position, post-structuralism and the *'WPR'* approach more specifically, in refusing to allow any comfortable spaces in which expert knowledge can be claimed to be purely and simply descriptive of some fixed state of being, provide an additional point of resistance to discourses which claim that today individuals who are on welfare, who are 'poor', are so on the basis of their individual developmental failures. They do so by insisting that such arguments do not merely describe a social reality but, through the classificatory choices implicit in scholarship practice, actively constitute social reality. This, in my view, is very much a space worth creating. I thank Carol Bacchi for her ongoing work in creating this critical space.

References

Altman, J. and M. Hinkson (2007) *Coercive Reconciliation: Stabilise, normalise, exit Aboriginal Australia*, North Carlton, Australia: Arena Publications Association.

Anaya, J. (2009) 'Statement of the Special Rapporteur on the situation of human rights and fundamental freedoms of Indigenous peoples as he concludes his visit to Australia'. Available HTTP: <http://daccess-dds-ny.un.org/doc/UNDOC/GEN/G09/168/88/PDF/G0916888.pdf?OpenElement> (accessed January 2011).

Bacchi, C. (1999) *Women, Policy and Politics: The construction of policy problems*, Thousand Oaks, California: Sage.

—— (2009) *Analysing policy: What's the Problem Represented to be?* Frenchs Forest, New South Wales: Pearson Education.

Bessant, J., R. Watts, T. Dalton and P. Smyth (2006) *Talking policy: how social policy is made*, New South Wales: Allen and Unwin.

Bletsas, A. (2010) 'Poverty in the "Age of Affluence": A governmental approach', unpublished PhD thesis, University of Adelaide.

Chia, R. (1996) 'The Problem of Reflexivity in Organizational Research: Towards a postmodern science of organization', *Organization* 3 (1): 31-59.

Coalition for Evidence-Based Policy (2011) 'Evidence-based Reform: A key to major gains in education, poverty reduction, crime prevention, and other areas of social policy', The Coalition for Evidence-Based Policy Website. Available HTTP: <http://coalition4evidence.org/wordpress/?page_id=6> (accessed January 2011).

Dean, M. (1991) *The Constitution of Poverty: Towards a genealogy of liberal governance*, London and New York: Routledge.

Dean, M. and B. Hindess (1998) *Governing Australia: Studies in contemporary rationalities of government*, Cambridge: Cambridge University Press.

Ferguson, M. (2008) 'Special Report: Aboriginal communities in distress over humbugging', *3rd Degree*, 6, 5. Available HTTP: <http://3degree.ecu.edu.au/articles/1987> (accessed January 2011).

Foucault, M. (1991) 'Governmentality', in G. Burchell, C. Gordon and P. Miller (eds) *The Foucault Effect: Studies in governmentality*, Chicago: University of Chicago Press, 87-104.

—— (2003) *The Order of Things*. London and New York: Routledge.

Gibson, P. (2010) 'Working for the Basics Card in the Northern Territory: The impact of the Northern Territory Emergency Response and associated policies on employment conditions in NT Aboriginal communities', Discussion Paper Jumbunna Indigenous House of Learning, Sydney: University of Technology.

Gordon, J. (2010) 'Job Seekers in Poverty as Dole Loses Buying Power', *The Age* 28 November 2010. Available HTTP: <http://www.theage.com.au/national/job-seekers-in-poverty-as-dole-loses-buying-power-20101127-18bjm.html> (accessed January 2011).

Hall, L. (2010) 'Income Card Failing to Prevent "humbug" in Tiwi Islands', *The*

Australian 13 February 2010. Available HTTP: <http://www.theaustralian.com.au/news/nation/income-card-failing-to-prevent-humbug-in-tiwi-islands/story-e6frg6nf-1225829865435> (accessed January 2011).

Hamilton, C. (2005) 'Poverty in Australia: Vinnies versus the CIS', *The Australia Institute Newsletter*, 44: 4-5. Available HTTP: <https://www.tai.org.au/?q=node/10> (accessed July 2006).

—— (2006) 'What's Left? The death of social democracy', *Quarterly Essay* 21: 1-69.

Hinkson, M. (2007) 'Introduction: In the name of the child', in J. Altman and M. Hinkson (eds) *Coercive Reconciliation: Stabilise, normalise, exit Aboriginal Australia*, North Carlton, Australia: Arena Publications Association, 1-12.

Inglehart, R. (1977) *The Silent Revolution: Changing values and political styles among Western publics*, Princeton, New Jersey: Princeton University Press.

Karvelas, P. (2010) 'Ken Henry Triggers Call for Increase in Dole', *The Australian* 11 May 2010. Available HTTP: <http://www.theaustralian.com.au/in-depth/budget/ken-henry-triggers-call-for-increase-in-dole/story-e6frgd66-1225864742670> (accessed January 2011).

Kearney, S. (2007) 'Bar Humbug', *The Australian* 10 August, 2007. Available HTTP: <http://www.theaustralian.com.au/in-depth/aboriginal-australia/bar-humbug/story-e6frgd9f-1111114149020> (accessed January 2011).

Lunn, S. (2009) 'Academic Questions use of his Research in Identifying Disadvantaged Areas', *The Australian* 28 November 2009. Available HTTP: <http://www.theaustralian.com.au/academic-questions-use-of-his-research-in-identifying-disadvantaged-areas/story-e6frg6n6-1225804763505> (accessed December 2009).

Macklin, J. (2009) 'Social Security and Other Legislation Amendment (Welfare Reform and Reinstatement of Racial Discrimination Act)' Bill 2009, Minister's Second Reading Speech, delivered 25 November 2009. Parliament House, Canberra, Australian Capital Territory. Available HTTP: <http://www.jennymacklin.fahcsia.gov.au/internet/jennymacklin.nsf/content/ss_legislation_amend_25nov2009.htm> (accessed December 2009).

McKnight, D. (2005) *Beyond Right and Left: New politics and the culture wars*, Adelaide: Griffin Press.

Needham, K. (2010) 'Abbott Spruiks Return to Howard Regime', *The Sydney Morning Herald* 18 August 2010. Also printed on TheBrisbaneTimes.com, Available HTTP: <http://www.brisbanetimes.com.au/federal-election/abbott-spruiks-return-to-howard-regime-20100817-128lx.html> (accessed September 2010).

O'Connor, A. (2001) *Poverty Knowledge: Social science, social policy and the poor in twentieth-century U.S. history*. Princeton New Jersey: Princeton University Press.

Ravens, T. (2007) 'Labor Politicians Call on Rudd to Roll Back NT Intervention', *National Indigenous Times* 26 November 2007. Available HTTP: <http://www.nit.com.au/breakingNews/story.aspx?id=13467> (accessed January 2011).

Saunders, P. (2003) 'A Self-reliant Australia: Welfare policy for the 21st century', Centre for Independent Studies Occasional Paper 86, St Leonards, New South Wales: Centre for

Independent Studies Limited.
Sullivan, L. (2000) 'Behavioural Poverty', Centre for Independent Studies Policy Monograph 45, St Leonards, New South Wales: Centre for Independent Studies Limited.
Travers, P. and S. Richardson (1992) 'Living Decently', *The Australian Economic Review* 25 (3): 29-42.
Wild, R. and P. Anderson (2007) 'Ampe Akelyernemane Meke Mekarle: Little children are sacred', Report of the Northern Territory Board of Inquiry into the Protection of Aboriginal Children from Sexual Abuse, Northern Territory: Northern Territory Government. Available HTTP: <http://www.inquirysaac.nt.gov.au/pdf/bipacsa_final_report.pdf> (accessed January 2011).

5 | Digging deeper: The challenge of problematising 'inclusive development' and 'disability mainstreaming'

NINA MARSHALL

> ...the intent is to dig deeper than usual into the meaning of policies and into the meaning-making that is part of policy formulation...the focus on methodology and application means that the ['*WPR*'] approach is easily adaptable to other settings. (Bacchi 2009: vi)

As Carol Bacchi makes clear, the '*What's the Problem Represented to be?*' ('*WPR*') approach offers 'both a novel way of thinking and a new way of analysing policy' (Bacchi 2009: xvi). The '*WPR*' approach aims to serve two purposes. Firstly, as a mode of thinking, the approach shifts the focus of analysis from policy as a 'problem solving' exercise, a technical, neutral and responsive process, to a mode of thinking that sees policy as an act which is constructive of 'problems', political and contingent. This enables us to call into question the 'problems' inherent in specific policy proposals and dig deeply into the meaning-making that they are both reflective and constitutive of. Secondly, as a form of analysis, the '*WPR*' approach provides a clear methodology, based around a set of six guiding questions, to enable application of its way of thinking across boundaries of policy context and content.[1]

Much of the development and application of the '*WPR*' approach to date has been in relation to domestic public policy, often, though by no means exclusively, Australian. This chapter explores what it can mean to embrace the approach's mode of thinking and apply its form of analysis to new contexts and forms of policy by reflecting on its application within my ongoing PhD research.[2] My research explores proposals for 'disability mainstreaming' and 'inclusive development' within international development policy through analysis of the World Bank's disability website. Beginning by outlining the thesis background, I then

---

[1] See for example Bacchi 2009: 1-53 for an overview of the '*WPR*' approach, see also Chapter 2, this volume.
[2] This work was supported by Economic and Social Research Council postgraduate studentship PTA-031-2005-00206.

highlight challenges that the '*WPR*' approach has raised in my research, firstly as a mode of thinking and, secondly, as a form of analysis. I argue, however, that elements integral to the approach itself have helped to meet those challenges. As a mode of thinking, the reflexive practice integral to the '*WPR*' approach has proven critical in the challenge of questioning concepts central to proposals for change linked to disability equality. As a form of analysis, the '*WPR*' approach's methodological flexibility has enabled it to be extended beyond its original borders in terms of both the content but also the context and form of 'policy' analysed. These experiences and the insights into the '*WPR*' approach they allow are suggested to be relevant as other researchers take up the challenge of digging deeper with the approach in new and challenging territory.

Disability and international development policy: The research terrain

International development actors, such as bi/multilateral donor agencies and international non-governmental organisations, have historically demonstrated little interest in disability and disabled people. Such organisations have tended to see these either as issues of charity, welfare or medicine that are outside their concern, or have restricted engagement to funding separate, specialist-run medical and rehabilitative schemes (Stone 1999a; Ingstad 2001; McEwan and Butler 2007). However, in recent decades, framed by two important UN declarations on disability,[3] mainstream development organisations have increasingly raised disability and disabled people as concerns in discussions that contain proposals for what should or could be done about related 'problems'. Today the Global Partnership for Disability and Development (GPDD) sees more than 50 donors, governments, academics, disabled people's organisations (DPOs) and non-governmental organisations (NGOs) collaborate around disability's inclusion within development efforts. A recent World Bank review found that all 34 of the major international and regional organisations and bilateral donor agencies surveyed included disability in either programmes or policies, declaring: 'disability has become a part of international cooperation and development aid' (Lord et al. 2010: 30).[4]

Many observers are more circumspect about whether such statements represent disability gaining a place 'on the agenda' of mainstream development, considered doubtful at least in terms of significantly changed practices (for example Albert 2005; Grech 2009). The extent and breadth of discussion of disability in mainstream international development has certainly increased, but only a handful of such statements constitute formal policy or strategy (for example USAID 1997; GDDC 2003; AusAID 2008). Most declarations of interest in disability have either an ambiguous policy status—issue or position papers, guidance notes, focus papers and plans (for example DFID 2000; NORAD 2002; European Commission

---

[3] The World Programme of Action Concerning Disabled Persons (1982) and Convention on the Rights of Persons with Disabilities in 2006.

[4] Surveyed institutions included UN agencies, the World Bank, European Union, and bilateral agencies such as the Swedish International Development Cooperation Agency (SIDA), the Australian Agency for International Development (AusAID) and the UK Department for International Development (DFID).

2003; SIDA 2005; Austrian Development Cooperation 2007)—or are discussion and research papers that raise disability as an issue, debating associated policy and practice, but are clearly not formal policy (for example STAKES 2003; Fischer et al. 2006).[5]

Since the mid-1990s, policy proposals around disability in development have increasingly revolved around the concept of 'inclusion' and the strategy of 'mainstreaming'. The opening page of the UN Convention on the Rights of Persons with Disabilities emphasises 'the importance of mainstreaming disability issues as an integral part of relevant strategies of sustainable development' (UN 2006: 1), showing how widely recognised these proposals have become. 'Inclusive development' has been described as the 'global development community's response' to disability (Barron and Amerena 2007: 6), not just in terms of what the UN termed the 'silent crisis' of disabled people's exclusion and marginalisation (UN 2003-4) but also the effects of that on national social and economic development. While 'inclusive development' is not easily defined (Barron and Amerena 2007: 6), and 'disability mainstreaming' is similarly contested (Albert et al. 2005: 13-14), these concepts have nonetheless become the focus of policy proposals. The World Bank review cited above found that disability was being included through a combination of disability specific work and 'mainstreaming/ inclusion/ integration programs' (Lord et al. 2010: 31).[6] Indeed, the GPDD, with the slogan 'promoting an inclusive society', describes itself as 'a global initiative to strengthen international cooperation to accelerate the integration of disability issues and considerations into mainstream social and economic development efforts' (GPDD 2011).

My research explores these proposals for 'inclusive development' and 'disability mainstreaming', specifically examining policy proposals articulated within the World Bank's disability website.[7] Positioning itself since the late 1990s as the 'Knowledge Bank',[8] the World Bank[9] describes itself as 'one of the world's largest sources of funding and knowledge for developing countries' (World Bank 2007b: 3) and is seen as the 'leader' of development (Caufield 1996: 1). Its influence is widespread through its lending but also through its research agenda and publications such as the annual World Development Report, which often establish the parameters and basis of development knowledge and debate (Mallaby 2004: 71; O'Brien and Williams 2004: 275). The Bank has maintained a disability website since the late 1990s, employed a disability and development team and advisor, and played an integral role in the GPDD's establishment and hosting. With interest in including disability expressed at the highest institutional levels (for example Wolfensohn 2002), the Bank has produced a wide range of documents on disability, although no formal policy or strategy has been

---

[5] For an overview see Lord et al. 2010.
[6] This reflects the 'twin-track' approach to inclusion, in which disability is both 'mainstreamed' in general development and a 'disability-specific' focus retained (see for example DFID 2000; Barron and Amerena 2007). The quote also demonstrates how 'mainstreaming' and 'inclusion' are often used interchangeably.
[7] www.worldbank.org/disability, hereafter referred to as 'the site' or 'the website'.
[8] See for example Wolfensohn 1996, where the former Bank president declares the strategic intention to become the 'Knowledge Bank'.
[9] Hereafter 'the Bank' and 'the World Bank' refer to the International Bank for Reconstruction and Development (IBRD) and the International Development Association (IDA).

adopted.[10] Thus, within the broader terrain of disability policy in international development, the Bank's disability website offers an opportunity to 'dig deeper' into proposals for change articulated by an institution in a powerful enunciative position within development that has demonstrated explicit, sustained interest in the issue.

It is against this general background and in this specific context that the '*WPR*' approach is being used in my thesis. Discussion will now turn to the application of the approach in that research, its contributions and challenges, beginning with its role as a mode of thinking.

The '*WPR*' approach as a mode of thinking: The challenge of problem questioning

Moving from a 'problem solving' paradigm to one of 'problem questioning' is central to the '*WPR*' approach's contribution as a mode of thinking (Bacchi 2009: xvii). The approach challenges the assumptions about neutrality, technicality and responsiveness that lie behind much policy research, providing a way to think about policy as powerfully productive and political. The '*WPR*' approach shifts the analytical focus from how to 'solve' problems to calling into question the problem representations within policy proposals themselves, destabilising the taken-for-granted knowledge involved, and opening up space for new ways of thinking about proposals like 'inclusive development' and 'disability mainstreaming' and their potential effects.

In discussing the contribution and challenges of the '*WPR*' approach as a mode of thinking within my research, I will begin by setting out how the approach helps address limitations and gaps in the 'mode of thinking' within the analytical account of 'disability mainstreaming' and 'inclusive development' provided to date. Secondly, I will discuss how this rethinking brings challenges through its questioning of a policy area in which concepts and debates central to disability equality are deeply embedded. Reflecting on this, I will finally argue that reflexivity's integral place within the '*WPR*' approach is critical in responding to the challenges that the approach itself—as a mode of thinking—can raise.

The existing academic narrative of disability in development is limited in extent, and scholarship on disability and development rarely converges or crosses. The relatively few works that address this subject in general (for example Stone 1999b; Yeo and Moore 2003; Sheldon 2005; Grech 2009) tend to emanate from disability studies rather than from development scholarship. A search for 'disability', 'impairment' or 'handicap' in the titles, keywords and abstracts of issues of 44 development journals published in 1996-2002 found 31 did not include these at all (Yeo and Moore 2003: 575-76). A recent search of nine development journals between 2002-2011 using the same criteria revealed, with a couple of exceptions, a

---

[10] Compared, for example, to the Gender Mainstreaming Strategy Paper approved in 2001, the four-year Gender Action Plan launched in 2007 and the six gender-related commitments announced in 2008 (World Bank 2011).

largely unchanged picture.[11] Disability is strikingly absent from development scholarship, a bias in the literature with potentially significant effects. As Grech (2009: 771-72) has pointed out, the 'West' has dominated the focus, assumptions and indeed production of disability studies research, which may mean interest in disability in the majority world is marginalised and that inappropriate, Western understandings and concepts are exported to its study.[12] Similarly, the bias towards accounts of disability and development informed principally by disability studies, rather than by a convergence of disability and development scholarship, may also delimit the ways of thinking and kinds of questions asked.

Within this general lacuna, the specific narrative and analysis of disability policy in international development is confined largely to a grey literature emanating from NGOs, DPOs and donor organisations (see for example Singleton et al. 2001; EDF 2002; Stienstra et al. 2002; STAKES 2003; Albert et al. 2005; Barron and Amerena 2007). This literature tends to be descriptive, mainly telling a story of progressive, evolutionary policy development in response to 'better' knowledge and understanding, and anticipating a positive outcome in terms of 'solving' the problems of disability in development. Four areas of knowledge change are frequently cited as central in this process: the rise of the social model of disability; acceptance of a human rights approach to disability; appreciation of the links between disability and poverty; and a change in the broader development focus to poverty alleviation and human rights. The literature sees these four refinements of understanding, coupled with action by the global disabled people's movement (DPM) and organisational/individual attitudinal change, as prompting, facilitating and, at times, restricting the changes in disability policy in international development observed. While problems implementing 'disability mainstreaming' and 'inclusive development' are discussed, their overcoming is essentially deemed 'a matter of attitudes, political will and practical know-how' (Final Report from Copenhagen Conference 2000, quoted in EDF 2002: 18).

This account is not only limited in scale and scope, but its mode of thinking is considered problematic. It fails to problematise three contested, political and powerfully productive concepts inherent in the proposal for 'inclusive development' and 'disability mainstreaming': inclusion: development: and policy.[13] Taking these in turn, inclusion is a term with a powerful resonance through its relation to the disability equality movement. As discussed further below, the globally-influential social model of disability, strongly associated with the DPM and associated scholarship, frames disability at its core as 'exclusion'. Thus 'inclusion' is integral to the goal of equality for disabled people. As McRuer has pointed out, terms like 'inclusion' and 'independence' are highly successful 'disability keywords', but their adoption by organisations like the World Bank can be seen as marking 'a necessary and liberatory end to [disability's] history' (McRuer 2007: 6) in ways which fail to consider what

---

[11] Eight of the highly-ranked journals chosen were surveyed by Yeo and Moore. While patterns in the number of articles were similar, a medical or health focus to those published was less apparent than in Yeo and Moore's findings, perhaps due to the choice of journal.

[12] See also Sheldon (2005) on different approaches to understanding disability in the developing world.

[13] For similar points see also Grech (2009: 774-75).

happens when they 'travel' and the uses they can be put to. Such appreciation of and critical attention to 'inclusion' is largely absent from the account of disability in development policy.

Secondly, that account also tends to depoliticise or de-problematise 'development', the other half of the proposal. Demands for inclusion of disability on the mainstream development agenda overlook the nature of that agenda itself, which numerous other groups are campaigning to fundamentally transform (Yeo 2005: 4-5). Development's role in producing disability is also largely unconsidered, with inclusion into the existing development agenda potentially leaving its ableist presuppositions and conceptual underpinnings unchallenged (Power 2001). Dingo (2007: 96), for example, argues that 'inclusion' and 'mainstreaming' may maintain and reinforce historic colonialist and ableist discourses, distracting attention from the 'larger neo-colonial and neoliberal project' which re-marginalises those purportedly to be included.

Thirdly, policy also remains largely unproblematised, pictured as a neutral, 'problem-solving' and largely technical process. The idea that policy can, and does, respond to and 'solve' problems on the basis of 'evidence' gathered by experts remains at the core of the account, reflecting the evidence-based policy paradigm Bacchi (2009) identifies as currently dominant. A typical assertion is that: 'To improve proposals and action for social inclusion in public policies, a scientific evidence base is urgently needed' (Berman-Bieler 2010: 373). Several papers at a 2010 conference on the future of global disability research shared the perspective that such research is required to provide evidence 'about what works' (Shakespeare 2010: 7) to 'inform policy, to inform practice, to challenge, to provide "minimum standards", to offer the best possible programmes to improve disabled people's lives' (Mulligan 2010: 10) and, for example, to 'provide government with *valid direction* for prevention and care' (Khan 2010: 44, original emphasis). As Miles (2007: 2) notes, strategies on disability in developing countries have also seen a 'narrowing of proposed solutions…discernible in the globalizing drive to find and enforce the simple 'Best Way' to solve problems, which usually coincides with the latest WENA [Western European and North American] trend'. 'Inclusive development' and 'disability mainstreaming', in their current ubiquitous status, are examples of this narrowing, totalising trend, but this process and the policy paradigm it is part of remain generally outside consideration in the existing account of disability policy in international development.

In contrast to these limitations in the existing account's exploration of disability policy in international development, the '*WPR*' approach provides an alternative 'mode of thinking' that is explicitly intended to deepen exploration of policy as constructive, enmeshed in a focus on 'the political dimension of "problem" creation' within policy making and its consequences or effects (Bacchi 2009: 4). Within this way of thinking it is possible to more critically interrogate proposals for 'inclusive development' and 'disability mainstreaming' and to question the taken-for-grantedness inherent in these proposals. It is also possible to explore the effects of the problematisations within these proposals, to consider what they do, what they enable and preclude, and what their effects might be. The '*WPR*' approach allows examination of how these problematisations construct disability and development in particular ways and with particular effects, countering the 'problem-solving' slant discussed above, as well as subjecting 'inclusive development' to the kind of analytical attention that the insights of McRuer, Dingo and others suggest.

As a mode of thinking, the '*WPR*' approach thus enables me to ask particular questions about proposals for 'inclusive development' that address the analytical gaps identified in the literature. However, while the '*WPR*' approach as a mode of thinking makes clear contributions, it also brings some specific challenges and it is these that now become the focus of discussion. Beginning by outlining the challenge of problematising proposals for change linked to equality campaigns, I suggest the concept of reflexive practice within the '*WPR*' approach's mode of thinking is central to meeting that challenge, enabling the asking of hard but important questions.

The '*WPR*' approach is a questioning, probing and problematising mode of thinking and this brings particular challenges when used in relation to concepts and proposals deeply cherished within an ongoing struggle for equality. 'Digging deeper' into proposals for change articulated by those campaigning for equality can raise uncomfortable questions and be open to significant challenge. As noted above, 'inclusion' has particular resonance in the campaign for disability equality, which in recent decades has been fighting hard to shift the perception of disability. The view of disability as a medicalised, individual attribute of 'abnormal' bodily function or structure, synonymous with impairment, is rejected. The shift advocated is to an understanding that disability is the 'outcome of social arrangements that work to restrict the activities of people with impairments through the erection of social barriers' (Thomas 2002: 40). The 'social model' of disability, strongly linked to the global DPM and (principally but not solely) UK-based disability scholarship, fundamentally calls attention to 'the ways in which physical and social environments exclude individuals with impairments from participation in mainstream society' (Barnes and Mercer 2005: 1).[14] In doing so, 'inclusion' becomes the goal of the transformation sought. DPOs and disability activists are at the forefront of demanding 'inclusive development', building on the logic that the social exclusion imposed on disabled people necessitates their inclusion throughout all levels and forms of development work (Barron and Amerena 2007: 15).

Scholarship is understood to have an important role in the pursuit of disabled people's equality and empowerment. The editor of a major disability studies academic journal recently suggested that global disability research should involve scholarship which is 'pluralist and academically rigorous but which responds to the priorities of disabled people and their representative organisations and agencies' and in which 'academics take seriously their obligation to work towards processes of political transformation inspired by disabled people themselves' (Moore 2010: 5-6). Closely associated with social model insights are also strong, though debated, calls for an emancipatory disability research paradigm that empowers disabled people through transforming 'the material and social relations of research production' (Barnes 2003: 6). This seeks to place researchers' expertise and skills at disabled people's and DPO's disposal, and requires research to have 'some meaningful practical outcome for disabled

---

[14] See also for example Barnes and Mercer (2004) and others in the same volume for an overview of the social model—or rather, given the wide-ranging debate within disability studies and beyond, the social model*s* (Sheldon 2005: 118; see also Priestley 1998).

people' in terms of empowerment (Barnes 2003: 12).[15]

The '*WPR*' approach would have much to say about such debates, but as a mode of thinking, grounded in post-structuralist insights about the contingent, contested, constructed and productive nature of knowledge, it can appear substantially at odds with the overtly political agenda demanded of disability scholarship. Destabilising and contesting concepts like 'inclusive development' and 'disability mainstreaming', advocated by those campaigning against disabled people's impoverishment, discrimination and marginalisation, might not appear to add much politically or practically to that campaign, or indeed may potentially undermine what are perceived as its progressive achievements. Bearing in mind Grech's cautionary note above, significant challenges are also posed by a white, Western academic like myself using an explicitly critical mode of thinking to question and destabilise policy towards disability in developing country contexts that I am neither subject to nor engaged in trying to formulate. How my critique relates to the 'lived realities' of either disabled people or policymakers, and its empowering or emancipatory potential, are thus significant challenges that the '*WPR*' approach as a mode of thinking opens up, especially for a researcher for whom political commitment to disability equality is a powerful motivator.

However, a concept intrinsic to the '*WPR*' approach itself provides a powerful counterbalance to these challenges: reflexivity, or more specifically, reflexivity as practice. A much-debated concept, with many differing interpretations advanced, reflexivity fundamentally involves a concern with subjecting the researcher's own positionality—both structural and conceptual—to critical attention.[16] Reflexivity's centrality to the '*WPR*' approach as a mode of thinking is obvious: following the six core questions of the approach, we are exhorted to 'Apply this list of questions to your own problem representations' (Bacchi 2009: 2; see also Chapter 2 this volume). Thus the '*WPR*' approach is a form of reflexive practice that involves actively subjecting one's own practices to critical attention and considering what these (re)produce—or *doing* reflexivity rather than simply *being* reflexive (Bacchi 2011: 35-38, 2009: 45).

This is a requirement that I take to be directed both towards those articulating *and* those analysing policy proposals. Thus the '*WPR*' approach as a mode of thinking not only demands active reflexive practice of the individual researcher examining proposals like 'inclusive development' and 'disability mainstreaming', discussed further below, but may also valuably inform the efforts of others seeking to influence the formulation of such proposals, including academics, NGOs and DPOs:

> …it is vitally important that we, as researchers or as concerned citizens, undertake to apply the full set of questions in the approach to our own policy suggestions and the problem representations these imply. To subject one's own problem representations to critical scrutiny in this way involves a form of *reflexive* research practice… (Bacchi 2009: xix, original emphasis)

---

[15] See also for example Stone and Priestley (1996); Mercer (2004).
[16] See Bacchi (2011: 33-35) for an overview of reflexivity.

Rather than being a damaging destabilisation of concepts and proposals advanced in the name of equality, the '*WPR*' approach as a mode of thinking carries an inherent demand for reflexive practice. That demand offers equality groups a powerful and important way to subject external proposals that apparently represent 'success' in getting their agenda adopted to the kind of 'hard questioning' owed to those on whose behalf they campaign (Bacchi 2011). By asserting that 'no concept or category is accepted as value-free and uncontested' (Bacchi 2009: 32), the '*WPR*' approach disrupts the taken-for-grantedness of *all* policy proposals, no matter how apparently progressive. Echoing McRuer above, this suggests we should resist perceiving the adoption of 'inclusive development' and 'disability mainstreaming' as an end point. The '*WPR*' approach's disruptiveness demands those campaigning for such policy approaches see associated programs as 'fields of contestation', highlighting 'the *ongoing political deliberations that give those programs meaning and shape*' and requiring the asking of 'hard questions' when they are taken up (Bacchi 2011: 31, original emphasis). The need to ask such questions—to practise this reflexive mode of thinking, to understand how our own acts are productive and the effects they have—is thus a critical requirement not just for those adopting or proposing particular policies, but also those campaigning for or advancing particular proposals:

> While not wanting to discount the challenges and resistances posed by groups of people who mobilize to press for change, we need, in my view, to consider more closely the shape of the challenges they pose, the ways in which they perceive and represent 'problems', and the reasons for this…we need to reflect upon why certain reform responses get taken up, why others get dismissed, and what happens to reform proposals in the process of being 'taken up'. (Bacchi 1999: 7)

Thus, far from adding little to equality campaigns, the '*WPR*' approach proposes a political, evaluative and reflexive mode of thinking firmly located on the side of those harmed by particular problematisations, but one which does not accept easy predictions about the effects of certain problematisations, or that we should except from consideration proposals that have acquired an authorised, self-evident status, whatever their source (Bacchi 2009: 44).

Of course this requirement for reflexive practice applies equally to the individual analyst conducting the research. This can prove challenging but also brings to the foreground issues of positioning that can be valuable in assessing the analyst's own problem representations and in countering the kinds of challenges outlined above. Given the necessity for evaluation within the '*WPR*' approach as a mode of thinking, the issue of one's own 'values, assumptions, presuppositions and political motivations' (Bacchi 1999: 10) is explicitly marked for attention. This requires a reflexive practice that is never uncomplicated, as the analyst is just as embedded and constituted within particular discourses as other subjects. This means that the task becomes to try to engage in 'Detailed introspection, a "consciousness turned upon itself"…[as] required political practice' by turning the '*WPR*' approach as a mode of thinking onto one's own problematisations (Bacchi 2009: 45).

In my project this has involved not only engagement with diverse perspectives, as recommended by Bacchi (2009: 45), but also an ongoing practice of reflexivity through repeatedly subjecting my own work to the guiding questions of the '*WPR*' approach. One specific challenge, for example, has been to catch myself in the act of presupposing particular (deleterious) effects to the problem representations I identify on the basis of their source. The World Bank has attracted broad and sustained criticism, with its policies and actions often denounced by campaigners.[17] The active reflexive practice built into the '*WPR*' approach has helped me more critically engage with my own inclinations towards such assumptions, with the silences in my own narrative and the alternative perspectives available, and with the kind of Bank I am (re)producing within my research.

Another challenge relates to how my research could (re)produce hierarchical binaries such as developer/developing, able/disabled, included/excluded and (re)inscribe assumptions about the agency of subjects positioned and constructed within those binaries. Simply the practice of conducting the research, and the ways I am doing so, has effects in terms of producing myself and others as particular kinds of subject: for example, outside 'knowing' observer, agentic 'unaware' policy maker, passive policy subject. However, by *doing* reflexivity—by engaging in reflexivity as a practice—I do not except my own positionality and interpretations from analysis, nor act as if I can somehow step outside of them to 'reflect' on them. Rather, through the practice or doing of reflexivity I produce myself as reflexive subject *within* the research process, a position which, as Bacchi suggests, is critical in helping me to consider how I 'may inadvertently be complicit in oppressive modes of governing' (Bacchi 2011: 36). This key task is aided, not hindered, by the '*WPR*' approach as a mode of thinking.

Overall, as a mode of thinking, the '*WPR*' approach is enabling a challenging but necessary and rewarding questioning of disability policy in international development. This process raises hard questions through destabilising concepts central to the disability equality campaign, but also facilitates an active reflexive practice that is argued to be of value not simply to the researcher but to all those proposing change in relation to disability and development.

As well as offering a mode of thinking for 'digging deeper' in this way, the '*WPR*' approach provides powerful tools to undertake this excavation by advancing a form of analysis centred on a clear methodological approach, to which discussion will now turn.

The '*WPR*' approach as a form of analysis: Flexible questioning in new contexts

Both in *Women, Policy and Politics* (1999) and *Analysing Policy* (2009), Bacchi not only outlines the '*WPR*' approach as a novel mode of thinking but also demonstrates *how* it functions by elaborating on (and demonstrating) the approach as a form of analysis. Through its (now) six guiding questions, plus the directive for reflexive practice, the '*WPR*' approach steers the researcher through the analytical process in a coherent yet flexible way that appreciates each project's individuality and the need to foreground particular aspects of the methodology dependent on the research focus. This section discusses challenges encountered in applying the '*WPR*' approach as a form of analysis—and in particular the challenge of applying it

---

17 For example the Bretton Woods Project (www.brettonwoodsproject.org).

beyond the boundaries in which it was developed. I argue that the methodological flexibility of the '*WPR*' approach enables these challenges to be met.

The '*WPR*' approach directs us to start with a 'concrete proposal' (Bacchi 2009: 3) and work backwards; in other words, begin with a particular policy, identify the problem representation from what is proposed (Q1; see Chapter 2, this volume)[18], and from there delve deeper into this problem representation's presuppositions, silences and effects through the approach's remaining five questions. Analysis thus begins with the selection of text(s) within which the policy proposal is articulated, which in my research is the World Bank's disability website, a sub-site of the social protection section of the Bank's main institutional website. I analyse around 105 individual webpages (around half of which are identical to each other) gathered from versions of the site published in 1999-2009 recorded either by myself or by an internet archive.[19] These webpages are multimodal—meaning that they do not simply consist of textual elements but also images, page arrangement and design, audio and video *etc.*—and hypertextual—meaning they are electronically linked to other pieces of text and are thus able to be 'read' in a non-linear way. I do not treat these webpages as a group of 'texts', instead viewing the website in its entirety as one single 'text' which is constantly subject to (re)publication and alteration but which nonetheless maintains a coherence and consistency in its function as a single, authorised source articulating the Bank's representation of the 'problem' of 'inclusive development'.

The '*WPR*' approach is thus being applied to material beyond the boundaries of its original development, both in terms of the content but also the context and form of policy proposals examined: a hypertextual, multi-modal, institutionally-produced text with no formal policy status. Dealing with each aspect in turn, I will argue that the methodological flexibility of the '*WPR*' approach enables this extension, considered a positive advance given the ever-increasing utilisation of such policy forms and contexts in processes of governance.

My analysis is not of the kind of domestic public policy that, for example, forms the core of *Analysing Policy*, nor of the articulations of a 'governmental' institution in the traditional understanding (i.e. the political institutions of national government). I am interested in the articulations of institutions involved in the global development project, some of which are associated with particular national governments, such as bilateral donors agencies, but many of which are non-governmental or inter/multinational organisations. This potential challenge—policy context—is easily overcome through the flexibility of the approach as a form of analysis: the conceptualisation of 'governance' underpinning the '*WPR*' approach broadens the contexts in which it can be applied as an analytical approach (Bacchi 2009: xx, 20, 26). Understanding 'governance' as the way in which rule occurs, or 'how society is managed, and with what repercussions for different groups of people' (Bacchi 2009: 25) by institutions that go 'beyond the state to encompass a wide range of groups, agencies and institutions' (Bacchi 2009: 275), the '*WPR*' approach opens space to consider the role of transnational organisations which are deeply implicated in governing in this sense. That the

---

[18] Q1, Q2 etc. indicate the specific '*WPR*' question, following Bacchi 2009, see also Chapter 2, this volume.
[19] The Internet Archive (http://www.archive.org/index.php), which uses automated website crawlers.

World Bank is a significant 'player in the general administration of societal relations' (Bacchi 2009: 26) is beyond doubt. Its lending policies and actions reach deeply into the societies of the global South, while its position as the 'Knowledge Bank' ensures that the Bank is central in the administration of relations within the international development community.

More challenging is the extent to which the texts I am analysing are 'policies'. As noted above, the Bank has no formal institutional policy on disability. Moreover, despite its visual branding under the Bank logo, its location within the Bank's website, and its copyright being attributed to the World Bank Group, every page of the disability website hyperlinks to a set of legal terms and conditions that state:

> Unless expressly stated otherwise, the findings, interpretations, and conclusions expressed in the Materials in this Site are those of the various authors of the Materials and are not necessarily those of The World Bank Group's Board of Executive Directors or its member countries. (World Bank 2010)

Many of the documents hyperlinked to within the site, including those authored by Bank employees and published by the Bank, contain similar phrases distancing the texts from any understanding that their content represents the Bank's formal position. As McRuer (2007: 5) notes, such statements place texts of this kind simultaneously within and outside of the Bank—they are produced, developed and published by the Bank and yet do not contain statements or opinions attributable to it. Given this ambiguous position, it might seem that a form of analysis requiring us to begin with 'policy proposals' could prove problematic.

However, the '*WPR*' approach suggests attention is paid to policies because they 'tell us what to do'—they are a form of 'prescriptive text' (Bacchi 2009: 34). The flexibility of this methodological injunction means that it applies not simply to texts formally recognised as policy, but to the full range of articulations of 'what to do' by policy-making institutions like the Bank. While the website might not constitute official organisational policy, it articulates clear proposals and problem representations in a collective document whose prescriptive function was made explicit on its homepage for a number of years: 'The purpose of this site is to raise awareness of disability and development issues. A wide range of topics will be introduced as well as links to publications and additional resources on this matter' (World Bank 2005; World Bank 2007a).

The '*WPR*' approach as a mode of thinking suggests we pay attention to the fact that this text is not granted official status and consider why the Bank simultaneously provides this 'prescriptive text' on disability and development and denies it formal 'problem status', an issue of silencing and problem representation production and dissemination that at least two of the '*WPR*' approach's questions would draw attention to (Q4; Q6 see Chapter 2 this volume). Thus, far from being unable to incorporate texts of this nature, the '*WPR*' approach as a form of analysis is flexible enough to accommodate material accorded a variety of formal statuses.

To my knowledge, Bacchi does not explicitly discuss analysis of texts' multimodal or hypertextual nature, yet I am applying the '*WPR*' approach as a form of analysis to such material. Multimodality is an interesting oversight, given that this is not restricted to digital media but also inherent in how more traditional 'texts' are produced. Many government-produced reports use photographs and illustrating graphics prominently, as well as features like pull-out quotes and other design elements intended to draw the reader's attention, as of course do texts associated with other 'players' in societal administration like think-tanks, NGOs, media and academic researchers. Such non-textual modes are often integral to the elaboration of problem representations, just as much a discursive practice or form of knowledge constructing the boundaries of 'truth' and producing subjects in particular ways as overtly linguistic practice. Indeed, to distinguish 'text' from 'non-text' in this way is an example of the kind of hierarchical binary that the '*WPR*' approach draws our attention to. There is no reason in this form of analysis that the 'almost endless variety and numbers of texts that could be selected' (Bacchi 2009: 20) should not include types of 'prescriptive text' not captured in more conventional understandings of the word 'text'.

The '*WPR*' approach is also flexible in ways that enable it to meet the challenge of analysing 'hypermodal' sources. When hypertextuality is coupled with multimodality, as within the website, this forms hypermodality, or the interaction of words, images and sounds linked together in complex networks (Lemke 2002). This idea of a complex network, a web of interconnections, resonates with Bacchi's discussion of the need for the analyst to understand 'the web of policies, both historical and contemporary, surrounding an issue' (Bacchi 2009: 20-21). While here the nature of the 'web' is of course somewhat different, this awareness of the situatedness of proposals seems helpful in extending analysis to more explicitly interconnected 'prescriptive texts'. There is also a resonance between the way hypertextuality is often used within websites and the concept of nesting—the embedding of problem representations within one another—that is part of the '*WPR*' approach as a form of analysis.[20] On many webpages, expressions or terms deemed significant or requiring explanation are hyperlinked to another section or page elaborating that concept or phenomenon. Thus, for example, the underlined phrases are hyperlinked as indicated:

> The World Bank's mission [hyperlink to page defining Bank's role and work] is to fight poverty with passion and professionalism for lasting results. In the area of disability, it is working to ensure full participation of people with disabilities in its development work, as well as within its own organization [hyperlink to page discussing recruitment and employment of disabled people within Bank]. (World Bank 2005; World Bank 2007a)

Such hypertextual links may indicate key concepts or terms that need to be subjected to the approach's analysis, as well as clearly assisting in identifying how the problem representation is embedded within a web of other problematisations and debates. The idea within the '*WPR*' approach of this chain of analysis, this repeated act of digging deeper, as well as the intent to explore problematisations across boundaries in time, space and issue area (Bacchi 2009: xx), seem particularly relevant when dealing with explicitly hypermodal contexts of problem representation.

Indeed it suggests analysis of such contexts may be significant. Hypermodal contexts seem to be important sites of mediation between different discourses and institutions. In

---

[20] See Bacchi (2009: 21) for an explanation of nesting.

Women, Policy and Politics, Bacchi suggests extending analysis to material generated by academics and professionals influencing policy by citing Nancy Fraser's description of these as providing '*bridge* discourses, which mediate the relations between social movements and the state' (Fraser, quoted in Bacchi 1999: 11, original emphasis). A website such as that I analyse, sitting as it does both inside and outside the Bank, arguably similarly provides a space in which mediation occurs through bridging between its own (potentially multitude of) authors as 'experts' and the broader policy-making institution, as well as being a site of discourses which, to echo Fraser, mediate relations between the academics, professionals and campaigners focused on the issue of disability (equality) and development and the Bank. This suggests the analysis of such ambiguous practical (hyper)texts may be particularly useful, and the '*WPR*' approach as a form of analysis is proving to be extendable in ways which allow it to facilitate this analysis.

Conclusion

Digging deeper with the '*WPR*' approach, both as a mode of thinking and form of analysis, is a rewarding but challenging exercise. In my research, the '*WPR*' approach as a mode of thinking opens up for questioning concepts which are central to an equality campaign, but in its refusal to accept the taken-for-grantedness of any concept, no matter how cherished, it also creates space for a reflexive practice that holds significance for all those interested in such change. As Carol Bacchi (2004: 130) has pointed out, 'it remains crucial to examine the ways in which dominant frameworks of meaning affect reform proposals if the reforms are to deliver on the promise of real and meaningful change'. In my view, it is precisely the impoverishment, marginalisation and discrimination experienced by disabled people globally that demands that *all* those whose practices are implicated in the production of this 'problem' adopt a mode of thinking that creates space for critical evaluation and incorporates reflexive practice. The '*WPR*' approach contributes importantly to asking and attempting to answer some of the 'hard questions' of digging deeper into meaning and meaning-making in policy processes and proposals related to equality campaigns.

As a form of analysis, the flexibility of the '*WPR*' approach also enables it to meet the challenges of engaging with hypermodal, institutionally-produced texts without formal policy status. Indeed, tackling such novel contexts, contents and forms has particular appeal for an approach overtly interested in challenging boundaries and broadening the object of analysis. With digital communications and new media working their way towards the centre of our lives and assuming a growing role in how governing occurs, the ability to incorporate their analysis within the '*WPR*' approach suggests positive avenues for its advancement or extension. Thus the '*WPR*' approach, as both a mode of thinking and form of analysis, offers much to researchers interested in breaking ground to dig deeper in unexplored and diverse policy terrains.

References

Albert, B. (2005) 'Finally Included on the Development Agenda? A review of official disability and development policies', in C. Barnes and G. Mercer (eds) *The Social Model of Disability: Europe and the majority world*, Leeds: Disability Press.

Albert, B., A. K. Dube and T. C. Riis-Hansen (2005) *Has Disability Been Mainstreamed into Development Cooperation?* Available HTTP: <http://www.disabilitykar.net/docs/thematic_main.doc> (accessed October 2007).

AusAID (2008) *Development for All: Towards a disability-inclusive Australian aid program 2009-2014*, Canberra: AusAID. Available HTTP: <http://www.ausaid.gov.au/publications/pdf/dev-for-all.pdf> (accessed April 2011).

Austrian Development Cooperation (2007) *Focus: Persons with Disabilities within ADC*, Vienna: Austrian Development Organisation. Available HTTP: <http://www.entwicklung.at/uploads/media/Focus_Persons_with_disabilities.PDF> (accessed April 2011).

Bacchi, C. (1999) *Women, Policy and Politics: The construction of policy problems*, London: Sage Publications.

—— (2004) 'Policy and Discourse: Challenging the construction of affirmative action as preferential treatment', *Journal of European Public Policy*, 11 (1): 128-146.

—— (2009) *Analysing Policy: What's the Problem Represented to be?*, Frenchs Forest NSW: Pearson Australia.

—— (2011) 'Gender Mainstreaming and Reflexivity: Asking some hard questions', paper presented at Advancing Gender+ Training in Theory and Practice, Madrid, February 2011. Available HTTP: <http://www.quing.eu/files/opera/conference_programme_final.pdf> (accessed April 2011).

Barnes, C. (2003) 'What a Difference a Decade Makes: Reflections on doing 'emancipatory' disability research', *Disability and Society*, 18 (1): 3-17.

Barnes, C. and G. Mercer (2004) 'Theorising and Researching Disability from a Social Model Perspective', in C. Barnes and G. Mercer (eds) *Implementing the Social Model of Disability: Theory and Research*, Leeds: The Disability Press.

—— (2005) 'Understanding Impairment and Disability: Towards an international perspective', in C. Barnes and G. Mercer (eds) *The Social Model of Disability: Europe and the majority world*, Leeds: Disability Press.

Barron, T. and P. Amerena (2007) 'Introduction', in T. Barron and P. Amerena (eds) *Disability and Inclusive Development*, London: Leonard Cheshire International.

Berman-Bieler, R. (2010) 'Inclusive Development: Paving the way as we walk', in T. Barron and J. M. Ncube (eds) *Poverty and Disability*, London: Leonard Cheshire International.

Caufield, C. (1996) *Masters of Illusion: The World Bank and the poverty of nations*, London: Macmillan.

DFID (2000) *Disability, Poverty and Development*, London: DFID.

Dingo, R. (2007) 'Making the 'Unfit, Fit': The rhetoric of mainstreaming in the World Bank's

Commitment to Gender Equality and Disability Rights', *Wagadu*, 4 (Summer 2007): 93-107.
EDF (2002) *EDF Policy Paper: Development Cooperation and Disability*, Doc. EDF 02/16 EN. Available HTTP: <http://www.iddc.org.uk/dis_dev/mainstreaming/edf_policy.doc> (accessed May 2008).
European Commission (2003) *Guidance Note on Disability and Development for EU Delegations and Services*, Brussels: European Commission. Available HTTP: <http://www.make-development-inclusive.org/docsen/GuidanceNoteEng.pdf> (accessed July 2008).
Fischer, A., K. Franke and M. Rompel (2006) *Disability and Development: A contribution to promoting the interests of persons with disabilities in German Development Cooperation: Policy Paper*, Eschborn, Germany: GTZ.
GDDC (2003) *Informative Note for the Management Committee: Guidelines for Italian cooperation on themes concerning handicaps*. Available HTTP: <http://www.dcdd.nl/data/1056027782507_Italian%20Guidelines%20on%20D&D%20(English).pdf> (accessed September 2006).
GPDD (2011) 'What is the GPDD'. Webpage. Available HTTP: <http://www.gpdd-online.org/index.php?option=com_content&view=article&id=1&Itemid=50> (accessed April 2011).
Grech, S. (2009) 'Disability, Poverty and Development: Critical reflections on the majority world debate', *Disability and Society*, 24 (6): 771-784.
Ingstad, B. (2001) 'Disability in the Developing World', in G. Albrecht, K. Seelman and M. Bury (eds) *Handbook of Disability Studies*, London: Sage.
Khan, N. Z. (2010) 'Disability Research in a Developing Country', paper presented at The Future of Global Disability Research Conference, London, October 2010. Available HTTP: <http://www.ucl.ac.uk/global-disability-research/downloads/Naila_Z._Khan_Dis_Res_Pres.pdf> (accessed July 2011).
Lemke, J. L. (2002) 'Travels in Hypermodality', *Visual Communication*, 1 (3): 299-325.
Lord, J., A. Posarac, M. Nicoli, K. Peffley, C. McClain-Nhlapo and M. Keogh (2010) *Disability and International Cooperation and Development: A Review of Policies and Practices*, SP Discussion Paper, No. 1003, Washington D.C.: World Bank.
Mallaby, S. (2004) *The World's Banker: A story of failed states, financial crises, and the wealth and poverty of nations*, New Haven: Yale University Press.
McEwan, C. and R. Butler (2007) 'Disability and Development: Different models, different places', *Geography Compass*, 1 (3): 448-466.
McRuer, R. (2007) 'Taking it to the Bank: Independence and inclusion on the world market', *Journal of Literary Disability*, 1 (2): 5-14.
Mercer, G. (2004) 'From Critique to Practice: Emancipatory disability research', in C. Barnes and G. Mercer (eds) *Implementing the Social Model of Disability: Theory and Research*, Leeds: The Disability Press.
Miles, M. (2007) 'International Strategies for Disability-related Work in Developing Countries: Historical, modern and critical reflections'. Available HTTP: http://www.independentliving.org/docs7/miles200701.pdf (accessed April 2011).

Moore, M. (2010) 'The Future of Global Disability Research', paper presented at The Future of Global Disability Research Conference, London, October 2010. Available HTTP: <http://www.ucl.ac.uk/global-disability-research/downloads/Michele_Moore_Presentation.pdf> (accessed April 2011).

Mulligan, D. (2010) 'What Are the Gaps in Disability Research? NGO perspectives…', paper presented at The Future of Global Disability Research Conference, London, October 2010. Available HTTP: <http://www.ucl.ac.uk/global-disability-research/downloads/Diane_Mulligan_Presentation.pdf> (accessed July 2011).

NORAD (2002) *The Inclusion of Disability in Norwegian Development Co-operation: Planning and monitoring for the inclusion of disability issues in mainstream development activities.* Available HTTP: <http://www.norad.no/norsk/files/InklusionOfDisability.doc> (accessed September 2006).

O'Brien, R. and M. Williams (2004) *Global Political Economy: Evolution and dynamics*, Basingstoke: Palgrave Macmillan.

Power, M. (2001) 'Geographies of Disability and Development in Southern Africa', *Disability Studies Quarterly*, 21 (4): 84-97.

Priestley, M. (1998) 'Constructions and Creations: Idealism, materialism and disability theory', *Disability and Society*, 13 (1): 75-94.

Shakespeare, T. (2010) 'The Future of Global Disability Research', paper presented at The Future of Global Disability Research Conference, London, October 2010. Available HTTP: <http://www.ucl.ac.uk/global-disability-research/downloads/Tom_Shakespeare_Future_of_global_dsiability.pdf> (accessed July 2011).

Sheldon, A. (2005) 'One World, One People, One Struggle? Towards the global implementation of the social model of disability', in C. Barnes and G. Mercer (eds) *The Social Model of Disability: Europe and the majority world*, Leeds: The Disability Press.

SIDA (2005) *Position Paper: Children and adults with disabilities*, Stockholm: SIDA.

Singleton, T., M. L. Breslin, C. Lewis and R. Metts (2001) *Gender and Disability: A survey of InterAction member agencies: findings and recommendations on inclusion of women and men with disabilities in international development programs.* Available HTTP: <http://www.miusa.org/development/resources/genderdisabilityreportt.pdf> (accessed July 2004).

STAKES (2003) *Label Us Able: A proactive evaluation of Finnish development co-operation from the disability perspective*, Helsinki, Finland. Available HTTP: <http://formin.finland.fi/Public/default.aspx?contentid=50655&nodeid=15454&contentlan=2&culture=en-US> (accessed October 2008).

Stienstra, D., Y. Frieke and A. D'Aubin (2002) *Baseline Assessment: Inclusion and disability in World Bank activities.* Available HTTP: <http://siteresources.worldbank.org/DISABILITY/Resources/Overview/Baseline_Assessment_Inclusions_and_Disability_in_World_Bank_Activities.pdf> (accessed August 2004).

Stone, E. (1999a) 'Disability and Development in the Majority World', in E. Stone (ed.) *Disability and Development: Learning from action and research on disability in the majority world*, Leeds: The Disability Press.

—— (ed.) (1999b) *Disability and Development: Learning from action and research on disability in the majority world*, Leeds: The Disability Press.

Stone, E. and M. Priestley (1996) 'Parasites, Pawns and Partners: Disability research and the role of non-disabled researchers', *British Journal of Sociology*, 47 (4): 699-716.

Thomas, C. (2002) 'Disability Theory: Key ideas, issues and thinkers', in C. Barnes, M. Oliver and L. Barton (eds) *Disability Studies Today*, Cambridge: Polity Press.

UN (2003-4) 'United Nations Commitment to Advancement of the Status of Persons with Disabilities'. Webpage. Available HTTP: <http://www.un.org/esa/socdev/enable/disun.htm> (accessed April 2011).

—— (2006) *Convention on the Rights of Persons with Disabilities*. Available HTTP: <http://www.un.org/esa/socdev/enable/documents/tccconve.pdf> (accessed December 2007).

USAID (1997) *Disability Policy Paper*, Washington DC: USAID.

Wolfensohn, J. D. (1996) 'Annual Meeting Address Oct 1 1996'. Available HTTP: http://go.worldbank.org/SA5WLZWH70 (accessed April 2011).

—— (2002) 'Poor, disabled and shut out', *The Washington Post*, 3-12-02.

World Bank (2005) 'The World Bank and Disability'. Webpage. Available HTTP: <http://web.archive.org/web/20051219043518/web.worldbank.org/WBSITE/EXTERNAL/TOPICS/EXTSOCIALPROTECTION/EXTDISABILITY/0,,menuPK:282704~pagePK:149018~piPK:149093~theSitePK:282699,00.html> (accessed January 2009).

—— (2007a) 'World Bank & Disability'. Webpage. Available HTTP: <http://go.worldbank.org/0GWEU0VOY0> (accessed August 2007).

—— (2007b) *World Bank Group: Working for a world free of poverty*, Washington DC: World Bank Group. Available HTTP: <http://siteresources.worldbank.org/EXTABOUTUS/Resources/wbgroupbrochure-en07.pdf> (accessed January 2008).

—— (2010) 'The World Bank Terms and Conditions'. Webpage. Available HTTP: <http://go.worldbank.org/C09SUA7BK0> (accessed April 2011).

—— (2011) 'Gender - About Us'. Webpage. Available HTTP: <http://go.worldbank.org/6MGA8V2TN0> (accessed April 2011).

Yeo, R. (2005) *Disability, Poverty and the New Development Agenda*. Available HTTP: <http://www.disabilitykar.net/docs/agenda.doc> (accessed May 2008).

Yeo, R. and K. Moore (2003) 'Including Disabled People in Poverty Reduction Work: "Nothing about us, without us"', *World Development*, 31 (3): 571-590.

6 Answering Bacchi: A conversation about the work and impact of Carol Bacchi in teaching, research and practice in public health

JOHN COVENEY AND CHRISTINE PUTLAND

This conversation was arranged between two academics, John Coveney and Christine Putland, (both of Flinders University, South Australia), who had collaborated on a number of teaching and research projects that had incorporated the work of Carol Bacchi.

John Coveney (JC):
What I wanted to do with this conversation was to talk about the way that we have used Carol Bacchi's research and to consider her contribution to our individual projects and our collective endeavours. Let me start by saying that it was you, Christine, who was responsible for introducing me to Carol Bacchi's books and papers. Could you talk about how you had been introduced to her work, and how and where you used it?

Christine Putland (CP):
Basically I started using it when I was writing my PhD thesis (Putland 2000). I was introduced to Bacchi's work quite late in the piece and I immediately recognised that it was very useful in terms of the particular point I had reached at the time. Let me put that in context: I was working in the field of public policy, informed by disciplines with a particular understanding of the world. My interest in study emerged out of my work practice rather than vice versa and I didn't have a background in studying social sciences. In fact my undergraduate experience was in the humanities. I had become frustrated with the lack of theorising I observed in much of what we were doing in practice, but when I turned to the public policy literature it didn't seem to offer more than a fairly mechanical view of policy development. It was usually informed by a general ideological kind of position about what was 'good' for people and/or choosing actions from a narrow range of options that were informed as much by habit as actual analysis of effectiveness. Out of frustration partly at the lack of exploration of

alternative approaches I returned to study and when I eventually came to do a PhD it was, in a way, an attempt to make sense of what I observed in the field in terms of a broader and more relevant range of theoretical perspectives. So in general I had a practical orientation to start with.

More specifically I was using feminist theory to interrogate particular public policy frameworks and the theories that inform them. I had been struggling to find a language to bridge the evident gap between talking about what happens in practice and the theories that are said to explain them. The difficulty I was having working in public policy was the point of entry for thinking about what is and what could be, the tendency to start from 'we know what the problem is, we simply have to define it clearly and then we can agree on how to fix it'. So the relevance of the available theories tended to be taken for granted. But what Carol Bacchi offered was a lovely concise way of taking the thinking right back to basics and theorising about why we even came to look at the so-called 'problem' in the first place, which led to thinking about it in a particular way and so on and so forth. I was able to apply this approach for quite practical purposes. But really it was that simple idea of asking certain kinds of questions right back at the very beginning so you had to question what you have always done.

JC:
So if I understand what you're saying it is that a lot of public policy work fixes on things like the policy cycle as if, somehow, a problem falls from the sky quite unproblematically, and then the policy cycle goes through steps like 'consultation', 'developing instruments', 'implementation', 'evaluation' etc. Your frustration was that policy cycles started at a particular point, but you wanted to go somewhere earlier or different from that.

CP:
Yes. I mean the idea of a 'cycle' itself implies you've got to enter at some point, and it was always assumed that it was fairly obvious where you hop into it. It tended to be 'we start from here' as a matter of course, but also that we tended to question things in a practical sense but less so from a theoretical perspective: how did the cycle come to look like this and what does not even appear on the cycle. So we debated a great deal at a level of second or third order of theory of action: whether you do that or this, and *how* you do something. For me the attraction in Carol Bacchi's 'what's the problem' ['*WPR*'] approach was the simple way it offered of linking these levels of thinking and critical analysis.

JC:
I remember that you brought Carol's ideas into a particular setting that you and I were involved in at the time; we were putting together a topic [course] for a Doctor of Public Health (DrPH) programme at Flinders University. This was a quite peculiar 'beast' because we wanted to demonstrate that you can do coursework at the doctorate level but it needed to have a certain kind of characteristic: it needed to demonstrate advanced level thinking. That's where you introduced me to Carol's work.

In that course we examined how the media (newsprint and broadcast) is so important to public health. Not merely in terms of getting public health ideas out to the public—for example, in social marketing and health campaigns—but something quite different. We were interested in the way the media constructs particular public health 'problems'. We asked the students to look at the way a particular public health 'problem' had been represented in the media and then to look at how it was represented by the public health community in the professional literature. We asked the students to compare and contrast those two perspectives.

CP:
As I said I found that Carol offered a very useful way of introducing critical analysis to students who had not had much background in this kind of thinking. For some of the students it came completely naturally as a more concise way to encapsulate what they had some experience of already. But for many students it was completely new and provided a very transparent way of understanding a critical approach. I think for some of the students it took some time to get their heads around what we were actually asking of them, and in applying 'WPR' [the '*WPR*' approach] they didn't really get much beyond that simple question of 'what is the problem', but for students without a social science background who had been trained in more black and white frameworks this was significant.

I think often when we gave them things to read they would immediately go to the health content or issue itself and their knowledge of the particular policy area because that's what they were accustomed to doing; whereas we were saying 'look it doesn't matter what it is, whatever we give you, what we're asking you to actually do is treat it in a certain way… interrogate it and see what that process throws up and what difference it makes to the solutions you might come up with'—because that was, of course, one of the really important things—'what difference does it make if you look at it differently, if you actually construct it differently and think about it differently?' I remember being quite surprised and very relieved at how effective it was, in particular for some of the students who had not been exposed to critical analysis in the past, that when they got it they often really latched onto it as something they felt they could use.

JC:
And many of them took that approach further into their studies. I know of a number of students who incorporated Carol's approach into their dissertations and used it…to analyse a particular problem—not as the 'problem' but as the way the problem is represented to be. And actually, I think it was the early work we did with them on the media that made it all so accessible. Because if you just take a piece of policy and say 'what is the problem represented to be?' that's not as useful as when you take a media approach to constructing a 'problem' and then compare it with a professional approach. Often the media has exaggerated a story or represents the problem to be one of moral outrage. The professional approach, on the other hand, tends to be more sober. Allowing students to compare and contrast the way a problem is represented to be in the media and in the so-called professional literature was such

a stark contrast many students 'got it'. And the questions that Carol asks—for example, what presuppositions or assumptions underlie this representation of the problem? (Bacchi 2009: 2)—allow the students to compare and contrast the different representations. I think it was an absolute brainwave and I think that was a credit to you.

CP:

I remember having conversations with them around some of the questions, like 'who stands to gain?' Those sorts of questions were really interesting because many of the students, quite reasonably, would immediately focus on the monolithic kind of 'bad guys'; it's always the drug companies—or politicians but usually it was drug companies—big organisations out there were the problem, nothing to do with how 'we' in public health have constructed problems and therefore offered inadequate or simplistic responses. As we talked about it more and more they became actually much more attuned to the idea of positioning—how you might be positioned differently in relation to 'the problem' as defined. I think that was a real eye-opener to a lot of them and it would actually allow them to think about close-up (including clinical) relationships as well as the more 'at a distance' ones that they were used to focusing on.

JC:

I think that was one of my insights into Carol's work. Before I used Carol's approach I did not find critical discourse analysis very satisfactory. Examples of it were often influenced by the work of people like Fairclough (1995). This version of critical discourse analysis was an approach from the point of view of 'so where is the old-fashioned power in here? Where are the monolithic powerbrokers: full of money, full of status?' Carol's work is very different. It's more nuanced. I think this is where her work draws on the work of Foucault (1980) because she asks you to look at what the problem is represented to be. She wants you to look for a different kind of power, which is often a power that we (as academics/professionals) subscribe to. It's a model of how things ought to be because this is an appropriate and reasonable way to behave. So in many ways we are implicit in representing the problem in a particular way.

This brings us to our current work and I wonder whether you would be able to talk about how your work at the moment embraces any of the work that Carol has done in this area?

CP:

Well I can answer that in a couple of ways. One interesting observation I've made recently was in relation to some work I've been involved in around the concepts of 'lay knowledge' or 'lay expertise', and what that means in terms of understanding public health 'problems' and 'solutions'. Recently we wrote up a paper dealing with this issue based on a research project which was not necessarily set up to focus specifically on lay knowledges. As part of a larger study we had asked some questions of people living in diverse locations what they thought the issue of 'health inequalities' was about, using a newspaper article on the subject as a prompt. We asked them what they thought caused 'health inequalities' as reported in the newspaper and then we later asked them to tell us what they thought could be done about 'health inequalities' based on their analysis. Leaving aside the assumed 'problem' status in our questions, we were interested to find that many people's views about how to address public health 'issues' were not necessarily consistent with their analysis of the problem, which, while not surprising, we argued raised certain questions for the public health field. But the point of interest in this discussion for me is that it highlighted developments in public health thinking on such issues that has occurred over the past decade or so. In the literature on the subject there has been a shift towards emphasising both the relationships between public health problem construction and policy responses, as well as the relevance of positioning in relation to the designated 'problem' necessitating wider thinking about 'knowledges' for example.

To bring it back to Carol Bacchi, it occurred to me that her approach to policy analysis has been instrumental in making these kinds of shifts in thinking possible. Her translation of complex ideas into ostensibly simple questions has meant that it has been more readily taken up, at some level at least, in a range of contexts.

JC:
I've seen Carol's work come through on a couple of fronts. One was where I was asked to examine a PhD thesis that had looked at the evidence given to a government committee on obesity and type 2 diabetes in a particular jurisdiction. The groups that gave evidence were from the food industry, varying clinical professions, and from public health organisations that are usually more overtly political than profession groups. The thesis used Carol's approach to examine how each of these groups had represented the 'problems' of diabetes and of overweight, and the repercussions of those problems. The thesis looked at what the committee actually recommended and you could see the real effects of the way in which the problems had been represented and the evidence that each of these problem representations had drawn on. Very convincing.

Another example was when an academic from Canada came and worked with me last year. She examined the public health promotion of physical activity for children and used Carol's approach (Bacchi 2009). Interestingly, she found that kids can't just have fun anymore; play has got to be utterly utilitarian—it's got to be 'aerobic fun'. Kids having fun from a curiosity point of view—doing the sorts of things that you and I did as children—no. Fun has got to be 'physically fun', it's got to be aerobic, and it's got to be calibrated so you can measure it.

CP:
And I've got another example of that in my current work outside of the academic context. I'm actually focusing largely on analysing and evaluating initiatives linking the Arts to health and wellbeing. This work occurs in a whole range of different arenas; sometimes it's in health care or health promotion, other times in community settings and so on. Basically it involves arts practice developed with health and wellbeing effects in mind. One of the things that we grapple with is the sense that to be relevant to public health it has to be seriously useful. So just as in your example it's not enough to simply have kids running around and having fun, similarly in arts programs the demand is to show certain kinds of instrumental benefits, the

ones that tie in with particular policy agendas. So the potentially more intrinsic value of kids being creative, having the chance to make huge dinosaurs out of papier-mâché or whatever because it's damn good fun, is overshadowed by the idea that it might develop certain skills and therefore be a vehicle for something more serious than mere enjoyment.

I was listening recently to an argument for providing more physical activity time in the schools because it will solve the obesity epidemic. As they were talking I found myself looking through a 'what's the problem' lens and hearing them paint this awful, depressing picture of what kids should do in order to be good, healthy kids, and save us all the worry. My mind immediately flipped to the alternative, thinking 'what if we stopped talking about it as you must do physical activity because it's good for you and simply said 'hey, kids, who wants to put on some music and do some dancing' or whatever. And the question of pathways to something 'useful' becomes one potentially interesting effect rather than the exclusive motivation. In the process we might discover other equally interesting effects, you never know. So that is my first reaction to your example. But I admit that when I am working in the Arts and Health field I tend not to refer to 'problems' at all for strategic reasons. I am more likely to draw on your work around 'pleasure' in public health, John (see Coveney and Bunton 2003). In public health we've started to talk about happiness in this way, because many people correlate happiness with healthiness, but we rarely talk about pleasure in the same way (except in a limited way in the mental health field) despite the obvious relevance. Pleasure is somehow not serious enough, and it doesn't offer itself up for nice 'hard' measurement.

JC:
This is the way in which pleasure is somehow always associated with a utilitarian outcome. In and of itself pleasure is regarded to be a bit irrelevant. In the physical activity example, pleasure is okay as long as it is coupled with aerobic activity which, of course, is seen as 'pleasurable' from a public health point of view.

CP:
…and which is in fact a strong motivator surely. Coming back to the 'what's the problem?' ['*WPR*'] I don't tend to use the term 'problem' at all because I'm often trying to shift thinking away from Arts and Health as being necessarily about fixing something. The classic line in arts and health is that it's not a panacea, it generally doesn't claim to solve problems, it may offer something different. The challenge is to articulate what this relationship between art and health might look like within a 'positive health creating' framework rather than a biomedical treatment or risk reduction one. Whereas if our starting point is always in terms of how it satisfies a health-defined agenda—i.e. fixing a 'health problem'—then we may never get to the point of being able to have other kinds of conversations about it. I know that in Carol's work 'problem' is not intended quite in this literal sense, but it has been easier not to use it nevertheless, though at some point I will do some more work on how the approach could be adapted for this context without running the risks I describe.

JC:

In terms of my own work, I'm often in the position of asking students to make more of their data analysis than they usually do. Students are often very good at the descriptive phase: writing down what they see in their data. I make the next layer 'What else is there?' easier for them by providing an analytical lens. So the Bacchi '*What is the Problem Represented to be?*' approached is a way of doing that. The Bacchi model and the questions that Carol poses are useful, these are thing like: What are the presuppositions or assumptions here? What's left unproblematic? What are the silences etc. (Bacchi 2009: 2; see also Chapter 2 this volume) Those steps are very useful for the students to follow.

So coming to some kind of conclusion, in relation to Bacchi's work what sort of impression do you think it has had on your thinking?

CP:

Well it's hard to say because of course you're getting so many impressions from so many different directions. I think what's different about her work is that it offers a methodology for taking apart both theories and practices, and can help to think about the links between the two. The straightforward questions that she asks are really helpful as a checklist. I can be working with a student or a practitioner in the field and they will pop into my mind as a way of helping them to analyse their own thinking and practice. I think her framing of the process as a series of questions was really inspirational because the questions forestall the tendency to immediately leap to a solution without having actually 'problematised' the assumptions.

It has had an incredibly wide application. I think when people think about it and they find it useful in one area it naturally translates into a whole range of different areas. I admit that in my current work I have not the opportunity or the need to engage with it at a deep level, but I think that it is still effective nonetheless.

JC:

I think for me the structure of the Bacchi questions (see Bacchi 1999: 13; see also Chapter 2 this volume) has been really important, mostly because I think the final question has direct implications for public health. The first questions are things like: How is the problem represented to be? What are the presuppositions here? And how are subjects constructed in this representation? In a sense, they are a kind of a humanities/social science exercise. That last question—How would the 'response' differ if the 'problem' were thought about or represented differently?—is I think a public health question. This is because it gives you the opportunity to say well, if we thought about it like this then there's a possibility for this particular development or this particular phenomenon. Because public health is in the business of trying to improve health then the question leads nicely into the possibility that representing the problem like in this other way would improve people's overall health and wellbeing. It's that last question that allows me to say to the students this isn't just an academic exercise; it provides the opportunity for us to pose other possible approaches.

CP:
Going back to my earlier examples about lay knowledges, many studies were asking about people's views of what causes health inequalities, but our introduction of the second part of the question asking them not only to interrogate the problem but also to ponder the policy responses that their analysis might lead to was less common. Aside from operationalising the idea of 'lay expertise' more fully, in my mind this is the kind of questioning that the 'what's the problem' ['*WPR*'] approach encourages: in particular the idea that thinking about how we arrive at the point of saying something is 'this' sort of problem is bound up with the ways in which we propose to take action in relation to our definition. But it is not necessarily, as it is often portrayed to be, a sequential logic. The fact that many of us, including those in our study, struggle with the nature of these relationships suggests to me that flexible conceptual tools such as those developed by Carol Bacchi are invaluable.

References

Bacchi, C. (1999) *Women, Policy and Politics: The Construction of Policy Problems,* London: Sage.
—— (2000) 'Policy as Discourse: What does it mean? Where does it get us?' *Discourse: studies in the cultural politics of education* 21(1): 45-58.
—— (2009) *Analysing Policy: What's the Problem Represented to be?* Frenchs Forest: Pearson Education.
Coveney, J. and R. Bunton (2003) 'In Pursuit of the Study of Pleasure', *Health* 7 (2) 161-179.
Fairclough, N. (1995) *Critical Discourse Analysis,* Boston: Addison Wesley.
Foucault, M. (1980) *Power/Knowledge: Selected interviews and other writings 1972-1977*, C. Gordon (ed.), C. Gordon, L. Marshall, J. Mepham and K. Soper (Trans.), New York: Pantheon Books.
Putland, C. (2000) Feminism and Citizenship: Re-imagining public and private perspectives on women's participation, Unpublished PhD thesis, Flinders University.

7 | Located subjects: The daily lives of policy workers

ZOË GILL[1]

I remember sitting in the Napier Building's lecture theatre at The University of Adelaide in Carol Bacchi's undergraduate course as she developed her '*What's the Problem Represented to be?*' approach to policy studies. I wondered at how it could even be contentious that policy solutions represented problems in particular ways that could be otherwise (Bacchi 1999)—her insights seemed so clear, so well argued, and so consistent with the way I understood the world. I also recall determining a few years later that the only way I would pursue my higher degree in Politics would be if Carol would agree to be my supervisor—which thankfully she did. This chapter, which is based on my PhD research, is, I think, an attempt to discern what the '*What's the Problem Represented to be?*' approach might look like in practice. Here, I both offer a synthesis of my key findings and explain how they stem from Carol Bacchi's groundbreaking research. In doing so, I hope, to pay tribute to Carol the teacher and mentor as well as Carol Bacchi the fine thinker.

In this chapter I use Bacchi's distinction between rational policy-making—the assumption that there is a pre-existing problem in the world that we can identify and solve—and a recognition that policies represent problems in particular ways that have effects on people and social relations (policy-as-discourse). The '*What's the Problem Represented to be?*' approach is premised on and develops this latter understanding of policy. As noted, in approaching my research I was interested in exploring what a policy-as-discourse approach to policy might look like in practice. More specifically, I structured my research through a series of interviews with women who had worked in the policy area of gender and education in South Australia from 1977 to 2004 in order to explore their understandings of and practices

---

[1] Dr Zoë Gill currently works for the South Australian Department of Health. She writes here in a personal capacity and her views in no way reflect the views or policies of the Department of Health.

around policy and policy-making. These women worked in a shifting policy arena in which the policy focus was, at different times, on girls, on access, on equity, on disadvantage, on social justice, on gender, and on boys (to name a few). As I and others have argued, each of these policy concerns constructs the problem of girls' education in different ways which have various effects on girls and on their relationship to boys (Gilbert 1996; Yates 1993 and 1996; Bacchi 1999; Taylor et al. 1997; Gill 2005; Hayes and Lingard 2003).

Interestingly, these insightful and incredibly imaginative women tended to describe the policy realm and policy in terms reminiscent of the traditional rational policy narrative (for further discussion see Goodwin, Chapter 3 this volume). Very rarely did their understandings and practices reflect a deconstructive approach to policy and policy-making. Their way of explaining policy and policy-making processes sat uncomfortably with my instinctive acceptance of the critical analysis of policy implicit in Bacchi's approach and with my readings of the broader literature on policy-as-discourse (Ball 1993, 1994; Taylor 1997; Taylor et al. 1997; Watt 1993/94; Marginson 1997; Bessant et al. 2006). Rather than merely accepting these policy workers' words as evidence of and support for the rational model of policy-making, I wondered what explained this similarity and why the deconstructive approach to policy only rarely appeared in these workers' understandings. I argue that this conundrum is resolved by the presence of multiple and competing discourses of policy and policy-making, of which the rational understanding of policy is dominant. This dominant discourse shapes policy workers' subjectivities, how they understand, think about and enact policy.

The intellectual contribution I offer is an understanding of policy workers as located subjects. They are not separate and distinct from the policy realm, but able to objectively reflect on and dispassionately describe this realm and policy-making. Rather, policy workers are a part of the policy realm and policy-making and the discourses that circulate around and form these phenomena. The way the policy workers' talk about the policy realm and policy-making reflects (and reinforces) the dominant discourses. The point is that though the policy workers are describing a particular conceptualisation of policy and policy-making that reflects the current way in which policy is generally made, conceptualised and theorised, this way of understanding and making policy does not always have to be the case. Policy and policy-making could be otherwise—other, subversive discourses exist and were occasionally enacted by the policy workers, though much less often. At the end of this chapter I briefly outline the types of alternative policy work I would like to see more of. Identifying and hence disrupting the dominant discourses of the policy realm creates space for these alternative understandings and practices of policy and policy work.

Policy workers as located subjects

Understanding policy workers as located subjects stands in stark contrast to the common understanding of policy workers within the structure-agency dichotomy, which assumes that the bureaucracy and policy workers are separate and distinct. Central to the structure/agency dichotomy is the assumption of the rational humanist agent. Davies (1991) offers a comprehensive account of the difference between what she terms the humanist agent and the post-structuralist subject. She suggests that central to humanism is a particular definition of the notion of human agency. Under a humanist ontology people are understood as having an absolute and unitary identity such that one can be 'true to oneself'. There is a 'notion of self-sufficient independence' and a 'separateness' associated with autonomy or agency (Mackenzie and Stoljar 2000: 6-7). A person's identity is set up in contradistinction to the collective. Indeed, 'society' (and structure) is seen as something that threatens individual identity: a person is understood as exerting their agency *against* society or structure.

Furthermore, and significantly, Davies argues that agency, within a humanist understanding, is understood as 'control', that is, as 'the rational controlling the irrational and emotional' (Davies 1991: 44). Through rational thought a person can achieve their own individual identity. This, in turn, is closely connected to the conscious/unconscious dichotomy whereby the conscious, rational decision-making processes should be protected from all unconscious, emotional and irrational desires (Davies 1991: 44). Of course, a good deal of feminist theorising is associated with challenging the dichotomies of rational/irrational, conscious/unconscious, showing how they are aligned with and reinforce the male/female dichotomy (Lloyd 1984; Gatens 1998a) and present rationality as gender neutral rather than sexed (Gatens 1998b). It follows from this insight that the humanist conception of agency and rationality, with its connection to these dichotomies, is at best not helpful to women.[2] As Mackenzie and Stoljar (2000) observe, autonomy is viewed with 'suspicion' by feminists who tend to understand it as stemming from a 'political tradition' that has been 'hostile to women's interests and freedom' (Mackenzie and Stoljar 2000: 3). This scepticism amongst some feminists about autonomy stems from the links between the concept and notions of 'individualism' and 'rationalism' (Mackenzie and Stoljar 2000: 3).

The point here is that these dichotomies, and hence this individualistic notion of agency, are constructions. They are themselves part of the discourses constituting contemporary social relations (Davies 1991). Hence, all of our desires and wants, whether or not they are described as conscious and rational, are formed through the discourses in which we exist. Given the rejection by some feminists of this humanist agent as at best unhelpful to women, it is important to reflect upon the consequences that follow when policy workers who identify as activists pursuing feminist goals embrace and perform a conception of rational agency. I argue that this performance of rational agency limits the kinds of substantive policy options considered in a particular policy area, such as gender and education. My argument here takes seriously Brown's (1995: x-xii) call for politically committed subjects to look at what it is within themselves, at the ways in which their subjectivity is constituted, that makes achieving emancipation so difficult. There is no essential individual identity that can be separated from its surroundings, context, or society. The post-structuralist understanding of personhood captures this well.

---

[2] I reject Patai and Koertge's (1994) criticism that such claims are dogmatic and broad sweeping. Their criticism assumes a lack of rigour in feminist critiques of the Enlightenment and notions of the individual and rationality.

In contrast to the humanist approach, post-structuralism understands people as having a subjectivity. A person's subjectivity is formed through being within discourses: '[w]e are constituted through multiple discourses at any one point in time, and while we may regard a move as correct within one game or discourse, it may equally be dangerous within another' (Davies 1991: 47). Thus, a person's subjectivity is changing and contradictory (Davies et al. 2006: 87-88). With this analysis an individual is not in a dichotomous relationship with the collective, but rather '[t]he individual is constituted through the discourses of a number of collectives as is the collective itself' (Davies 1991: 43). Crucial to this conception is that there is no 'essential' self. A person's subjectivity, rather, is constituted through the available discourses (Davies 1991: 42-43).

The dominant discourse of policy workers as separate and distinct from the policy realm in which they work appears within the traditional rational policy literature (Hill 2003; Lipsky 1980; Kingdon 2003), as well as the more innovative policy-as-discourse literature (Ball 1990, 1993, 1994; Bowe et al. 1992; Yeatman 1998b; Taylor 1997, 2004; Taylor et al. 1997), and the femocrat, policy activist and social movement literature (Yeatman 1998a; Pringle and Watson 1992; Eisenstein 1996; Kenway 1990; Franzway et al. 1989; Malloy 2003). Wherever these theorists fall on the spectrum—or wherever they place their emphasis—policy work is assumed to occur within a structure that exerts power over or coerces particular actions. To achieve their own agendas, policy workers must push against these bureaucratic processes. These accounts of policy workers function within a structure-agency dichotomy. This way of conceptualising policy workers tends to mean that they are understood as separate from or outside of the policy realm. Indeed, we see titles of books such as *Inside Agitators* (Eisenstein 1996), *Activism and the Policy Process* (Yeatman 1998a) and *Between Colliding Worlds* (Malloy 2003). These titles express the assumption in this scholarship of the independence or separateness of the policy worker from the policy realm that, I argue, leaves part of the story untold. Specifically, this literature does not address the ways in which policy workers are constituted *within* the policy realm.

Generally, the policy workers I interviewed also spoke in the same way, that is, they assumed the structure-agency dichotomy. While there were very occasional instances in the interviews when the policy workers' articulated a sense of being shaped by and within the bureaucracy, which I elaborate below, they predominantly conceptualised themselves as strategically fighting against the bureaucratic processes in which they found themselves. With respect to the structure side of the dichotomy, they assumed that the bureaucracy imposed external constraints on policy workers. In these moments, policy workers were produced as mere advisors or implementers of policy, as 'busy little workers' and pawns to the 'mediocrity' of the bureaucracy, but not as *makers* of policy. This perspective appeared in the policy workers' understandings of policy as coming from elsewhere and directing their work, and of changes in funding requirements, departmental structures and policy imperatives coming from above and hindering their work, as well as in their work practices of seeking approval and following directives from above. Thus, the policy workers described times when they had little personal control over policies.

Importantly, however, these constraints experienced by the policy workers were conceptualised as contemporaneous with the very same policy workers attempting to manoeuvre around these constraints. The restrictions of the policy realm, therefore, were assumed by the policy workers to be *external* to them and their agenda. Indeed, the same policy workers conceptualised themselves as strategically manoeuvring around the policy realm to achieve their feminist agenda, reflecting the agency side of the dichotomy. In these moments, the policy workers understood themselves as the agential shapers of policy. Policy workers, therefore, became simultaneously 'busy little workers' *and* 'activists' within the policy realm. In both instances, policy workers are portrayed as agents separate from the policy realm, either constrained by or manoeuvring around the bureaucracy.

The point here is not to deny that, at times, the policy workers did indeed seek approval or follow directives 'from above' and strategically manoeuvred around policy constraints. There were certainly moments when the policy workers performed as 'busy little workers' and pawns to the 'mediocrity' of the bureaucracy, as well as times when they actively pursued their own feminist agendas. The interest here instead is to identify how these understandings and practices became part of a taken-for-granted way of conceptualising the policy realm and the place of policy workers within it. Such conceptualisations, or subjectivities, reflect and reinforce the conviction that policy workers are separate and distinct from the policy realm, obscuring the ways in which the policy workers internalised and interiorised the discourses of the policy realm, and constructions of specific policy problems. In contrast, I call for an understanding of the policy realm as discourses that shape the subjectivities—the thoughts and, importantly, the practices—of policy workers. Policy workers are not preformed individuals who arrive at the policy realm to either robotically perform the directives of those above or to fight against these directives. Rather, they are located subjects: formed through the environment in which they work.

The very act of recognising the taken-for-granted nature of the dominant discourse of the policy realm goes some way towards disrupting it. Dominant discourses can be subverted and fractured. The discourse of policy workers as strategic agents manoeuvring within and against the bureaucracy was occasionally, although not often, challenged by the policy workers themselves. There were brief moments when the policy workers identified their locatedness within the policy realm. For example, one policy worker felt that the bureaucracy affected the ways in which the policy workers behaved:

> And what was scary though, for me, was I found myself acting like a naughty girl. I'd be really cheeky, and just naughty. You'd get really—I used to wear a [jump] suit, the kids used to call it the clown suit…I'd wear that to work. I mean I look back on it…!

Contrary to this worker's statements about choosing to be 'naughty' so as to strategically manipulate the bureaucracy, there was a sense in the quote above that she had become a 'naughty girl' because of the ways in which policy workers were constructed as agitators in the department. This sense of the interrelationship of the policy worker and the policy realm, I argue, needs to be developed further to address how the discourses around and in the policy realm itself, the assumption of the rational humanist agent, shapes policy workers.

The subjectivities of policy workers and the implications for policy practice

The taken-for-granted nature of the structure-agency dichotomy and its centrality in established rational constructions of policy and policy-making has effects that I argue need to be challenged. Specifically, it produces a particular kind of subjectivity in policy workers: that of the active, strategically engaged agent of change who identifies pre-existing problems in the world and attempts to solve them. I argue for an understanding of the located position of policy workers because, as will become clearer below, this will produce different types of policy workers who undertake policy work that recognises the discursive effects of substantive policies on people and social relations.

The policy-as-discourse theorists (Bacchi 1999: 45; Marginson 1997; Popkewitz and Lindblad 2000; Popkewitz 1998: 1; Ball 1993: 14) offer fundamental insights about the effects of policies as discourses, particularly Marginson's (1997) work on the effects on people of policy discourses. He offers a good example of the way in which substantive policy discourses create subjectivities. In his discussion of higher education, he argues that, as the human capital approach to education became increasingly dominant, through policies like the Higher Education Contribution Scheme (HECS), students began (reasonably) to think of their education as an investment and acted accordingly. As Marginson writes:

> [w]hen governments imagine students to be financial investors in their own economic futures, and consistent with this vision, provide student financing in the form of student loans repayable after education, forcing students to take into account their future earnings when choosing their course, more of those students *become* self managing investors in themselves. These economic behaviours are never as complete as the theory imagines. The student subjects also have other identities and behaviours, and no one is ever completely 'governed'. Nevertheless, the point is that joined to government, [the discourse of] the economics of education forms the objects of which it speaks. It produces itself as true. (Marginson 1997: 225, original emphasis)

Marginson, and others (see, for example, Shore and Wright 1997: 4, 6 and 29-34; Bacchi 2004; Ball 2003; Maclure 2006), have shown how particular substantive policy discourses create specific subjectivities. However, little has been said about the ways in which the discourses that shape the policy realm also create particular subjectivities (in policy workers). While Marginson highlights the subjectivities created in students by human capital approaches to higher education, I argue that the policy realm that values agency creates particular subjectivities in policy workers. The question becomes, what sort of subjectivities are created by the acceptance of the structure-agency dichotomy? As indicated, the ideal policy worker, both in the literature and in the case study, is that of the humanist agent. The structure/agency dichotomy, assumed in both these realms, constructs policy workers as separate and distinct from the policy realm and as rational and agential individuals. Importantly, it is assumed that policy workers can (in agential fashion) identify and solve (rational) pre-existing problems; they perform rational policy work. In other words, the model policy worker becomes, to borrow Popkewitz's expression in a slightly different but related context, 'an active entrepreneurial self, a decentralized citizen who is active, self-motivated, participatory, and problem solving' (Popkewitz 1998: 12). For example, the policy workers in my case study described times when they 'identified' the problem of girl's education and 'fought' to embed their solutions in specific policy directions without reflecting on the discursive effects of those policy solutions, such as valuing and reinforcing traditional masculine ways of being or constructing boys and girls as in competition (Gill 2005).

As Marginson and Davies point out above, subjectivities are never complete, nor are they necessarily consistent. Policy workers are not, as the traditional approach would suggest, *completely* rational agents. The significance of recognising that subjects have multiple and contradictory identities and behaviours is that these alternative subjectivities draw attention to how the accepted models of policy work and policy workers replace other ways of doing policy and other ways for policy workers to be. There are other subjectivities available for policy workers—as reflexive, reflective, and critical policy workers. Policy workers can be located subjects who understand policy-as-discourse. We saw above, that there were brief instances when the policy workers of my case study identified their locatedness within the policy realm. At the end of this chapter, I provide an example of a policy worker reflecting on the discursive nature of policies. This alternative understanding of policy workers as located subjects deserves support, I suggest, because in the long run it will encourage recognition of the constructed and constitutive character of specific policies.

To argue that the policy realm constructs policy workers' subjectivities is to say something about the way in which policy workers undertake their work. Discourses are found in and are formed by words and texts, as well as actions and practices. Words are important here as they reveal the ways in which we understand the world. But the way that the policy workers talk about policy reflects how policy is *done*. And looking at what they say tells us something about policy *practice*. Practice is the material instantiation of discourses (Burr 2003: 63). Understanding discourses as practices avoids the common question of whether practices come before discourses or discourses come before practices: they are part of the same thing.

Practices are understood here as embodied discourses. For example, policy workers who passionately search for more accurate understandings of the problem of girls' inequality or who pride themselves on being 'efficient' embody the rational model of policy-making: witness the 'burn out and stress' they experience (Eisenstein 1996: 207). With Bacchi and Beasley (2005: 190; see also Chapter 8, this volume), I wish to avoid a sense of 'talking heads' under which discourses are located in the symbolic realm and outside of the embodied person. Understanding discourses as practices (Burr 2003: 63) clarifies the point. To claim that discourses (practices) create and reflect subjectivities is precisely to claim that discourses are embodied, that is, that they produce *embodied* subjectivity (Rothfield 1992: 41, and 45-46), affecting the 'material body' (Davies et al. 2006: 90). A person's subjectivity has consequences not only for how they think, but also for how they act: it shapes 'who they are' (Ball 2003: 215). Drawing on Butler's (1999) notion of gender performativity, I understand policy workers as *performing* rational, agential policy not because they freely and consciously choose to do so, but because it makes sense to act in this way: the policy workers hold a rational, agential subjectivity. The structure/agency dichotomy and its assumption of the rational humanist agent suggests a practice of policy that involves research and data collection and associated attempts to understand problems accurately, as well as strategic, opportunistic work. In all these ways policy workers *perform* as rational agents—they have internalised and interiorised the humanist agent.

My concern with practices differs from the way in which the issue of practice is addressed within traditional policy literature. I step outside conventional frameworks that pit agents against structural constraints and conceptualise policy practices as the result of either constraints or agency. 'Constraints' on practice, in this approach, would include the location of the gender unit within the department, the number of staff, the extent of available resources, and the processes of reporting. Practices described as 'agential acts' would include activities such as networking, framing arguments, and strategic manoeuvring. In my view, these 'constraints' and 'acts of agency' do not in some straightforward way shape what can be done. Rather, the conceptualisation of these practices as the result of either 'constraints' or 'agency' actively constitutes policy workers' subjectivities as rational agents, separate from and fighting against the policy realm. Subjectivities are formed through and reflected in small daily routines (Burr 2003: 76) or social practices (Popkewitz 1996: 28). These small daily routines and how they are understood *are* discourses of the policy realm. For example, rationality and agency are enacted in such practices as the writing of briefing papers, seeking approval from those in authority, strategic manoeuvring, shaping policy focuses, networking, quantitative data collection, following instructions, working fast to time lines, evaluating policy against stated objectives, and working with policy language from above.

My case study offers insights into the nuances of the enactment of rational agential policy work. With respect to the agency side of the humanist agent, the policy workers generally emphasised their ability to conduct strategic policy work. They highlighted struggles and small victories—and obscured points of consensus—both in terms of assumptions about the humanist agent and in terms of particular policies. This strategic policy work entailed a particular type of policy worker. That is, in the case study policy workers were constructed as particular types of people: in the various policy workers own words they were 'sassy', 'caped crusaders', 'opportunistic', 'clever', 'mavericks', 'fleet of foot', and 'activists' who could 'do anything'. They could shape the policy agenda. Indeed, they were the 'enemy within'. One of the workers suggested, with a sense of pride shared by the other policy workers, that to work in the gender and education policy area 'you need intellectual engagement as an educationalist and strategic nous and courage and bureaucratic and policy adroitness'. This perspective manifested in the policy workers' understandings of themselves as 'getting things done' and 'making things happen', in the ways in which they fought for and defended their feminist interests against the policy realm as a whole, and in how they attempted to use the bureaucracy for their own purposes.

The policy workers at times embraced the bureaucratic processes as a competitive game that they could 'win'. For example, one of the workers talked about the need to take proposed policies 'through all the processes', and to get proposals past senior management. However, she also emphasised her strategic work: 'But basically it was both a mixture of be good enough and be sassy enough to get the in-principle approval and then roll really fast with it. Not dither around and decide what you were going to do'. She described the strategy needed to get the in-principle approval from above and then 'running and knitting it into something as you went along'. So we can see here that she saw herself as strategically working for her preferred policies, which locates policy workers as agential within, though manoeuvring around, external barriers imposed by the policy realm. Yet, this worker held a sense of pride in the policy workers' ability to work fast and gain the approval from above: she had partly embraced the policy-making processes of a hierarchical bureaucracy and her ability to 'win' within these processes.

Ironically, in the very act of emphasising their strategic policy work, the policy workers obscured the ways in which they shared assumptions with the bureaucracy, both in terms of the assumption of the structure-agency dichotomy and in terms of policies as rational responses to pre-existing problems. The way one of the policy workers answered my question about how she felt regarding her achievements during her time in the gender and education unit illustrates this point well. Her answer reveals her overall sense of agency within the policy realm:

> I feel very good about the three years I spent in there. I think I did profoundly well, with getting other people, I mean I didn't do it by myself, but in a sense I did it by myself in that I found other people to do it. …I eventually got permanent staffing in the unit, there were people in there. And that was [name], the Deputy Director-General of resources, because he decided I was a good egg. And in the year of the worst budget they'd ever had in the education department I was the only person who got staff. And they all kept on saying 'how did this happen?' and I said, 'you kept on trying to persuade the wrong person'. I cottoned on to the fact of who held the money and was lovely to [the Deputy Director-General] and wrote him a beautiful speech to talk to the Primary Principles Association about…girls' education. So I reckon we did a lot. Certainly the positive discrimination thing was important legally and historically, it was highly contentious.[3] The range of initiatives that there were in relation to maths and science education, to subject choice, to what readers we used in the early years of school. A whole lot of things changed there. We had somebody permanently working on the big project for the secondary social science curriculum, somebody permanently working…on the maths curriculum, about trying to work through…where there were probl[ems]…I mean that whole issue of, is maths itself inimitable to girls? Or, is it the kinds of examples that are used? Should you be teaching differently? We did quite a lot of…on the ground research about teaching practices. And certainly by the time I left, there was a unit, I mean there was a group of people whose job it was to be…working in the curriculum development processes of the education department. Well, that's not bad in three years.

This worker had effectively manipulated the hierarchical structures of the bureaucracy by gaining the support of key people, so as to increase staffing levels, which in turn allowed the unit to focus on a number of areas. Further, the areas she decided to focus on were at her discretion. This worker conceptualised herself as an agential policy worker manipulating the bureaucracy for her purposes. However, there was no reflection on how the areas or questions

---

[3] This was a reference to s 47 of the *Equal Opportunity Act 1984* (SA), which allows schools to employ women teachers in specified circumstances.

that were addressed were constructed in the first place. Many of the areas listed by this policy worker as requiring intervention—'positive discrimination', 'maths and science', 'subject choice'—construct the problem of gender and education in particular ways (Bacchi 1999). For instance, such policies problematise girls and their choices and reinforce boys' pathways as the norm. The assumption of the rational agential humanist agent draws attention away from the construction of specific policy problems. Or, in other words, the emphasis on entrepreneurial policy activism leads to policy work that obscures the way in which gender and education policies construct boys and girls in particular ways.

The policy workers all placed much emphasis on the individual policy workers' strategic manoeuvring within the policy realm to achieve their agendas. Such a conceptualisation leaves little place for other ways of being. There is limited space (or time) in this construction of policy workers for the reflexive and reflective policy worker who considers their own location within the policy realm and then considers the discursive character and effects of policies, which is the kind of policy worker I imagined.

In fact, the situation in the case study is quite the opposite. The policy workers had also internalised the rational side of the humanist agent: they assumed that problems existed independently in the world and could be solved. This understanding sits in stark contrast to the fundamental premise in Bacchi's '*What's the Problem Represented to be?*' approach—that problems are not exogenous to policy. For example, when I asked one of the workers whether policies responded to problems that existed in an objective world or whether it was something different from this she acknowledged the complexity of the issue but ultimately felt that there were real issues that needed addressing:

> [F]rom where I sat and sit, there were a number of national reports that were really important that *identified* that girls weren't participating, weren't having the same outcomes as boys…*they were just big sort of facts* that were *revealed* through these studies and clearly someone who initiated the studies was already working on a *whole lot of information that had been coming forward about the fact* that girls and women were not there in terms of school outcomes, post-school options. And all of that stuff was happening in light of other movements that were going on in relation to feminism…And so I think they all came together…so there was the support…for those issues to be raised and addressed. …And then the people who worked in those areas, who would have contributed to the *fact* that they…*needed* to be dealt with, then those people furthered the whole idea of 'the policy'. *Because clearly there needed to be something done because the whole situation was completely inequitable.* (Emphasis added)

There are assumptions in this worker's comments about policies responding to pre-existing 'facts' that had been 'identified' and 'revealed'. However, she unquestioningly talked about these 'facts' in terms of 'participation', 'outcomes', and 'post-school options' for girls, obscuring the ways in which framing the issues in these ways problematised girls (Taylor et al. 1997) and obscured the valuing and advantage of boys (Eveline 1994). As others have observed, the way in which the education of girls and boys is talked about represents the problem in particular ways that has effects on people and social relations (Bacchi 1999; Yates 1993).

This dominant discourse of rational policy-making produced policy work that failed to engage with the deeply embedded nature of values in policies, that evaluated policies in limited ways, and that overlooked the impact of framing policies in specific terms. With respect to values, the assumption of the rational policy worker can be seen in the way in which the policy workers conceptualised values in the policy realm as always readily identifiable and either as easily put aside or as purposively defended. This created policy work directed at identifying needs, looking for 'advances' in theoretical understandings, and searching for accurate research and data. It also meant that the policy workers felt that policies that did not address the 'real' issues, such as the focus on boys and education, were merely ineffective. I, along with the policy-as-discourse theorists referred to above, suggest that policy framings or problem representations have much more pervasive, discursive effects. The policy focus on the education of boys, for example, has led to a reclaiming of traditional masculinity and framed girls and boys as in competition (Gill 2005).

Further, the policy workers in the case study evaluated policies against their stated objectives or according to the purposive practices of teachers. The emphasis on the stated objectives of policies is evident in the ways in which the policy workers talked about policies as identifying and attempting to solve problems, and in the way they looked for techniques to facilitate the accurate implementation of policies and espoused the articulation of measurable 'outcomes' for policies. Missed here are the broader discursive effects of policies, the ways in which policies shape social relations, exclude, categorise and silence some people, and leave some issues unaddressed.

Lastly, the policy workers in the case study conceived of policy language and focuses variously as describing reality, as superficial—and hence to be manoeuvred around—or as aligning in some straightforward way with particular articulated interests. I suggest these conceptualisations of language reflect an underestimation by the policy workers of the impact of policy language, focuses and ideas. They obscure the productive character of policy language, concerns and concepts, and neglect the constructed and constitutive character of policies. Words and concepts, as part of policy discourses, shape the ways through which we make sense of the world.

My purpose in identifying the discourse of the humanist agent in the literature and in my case study is to disrupt traditional ways of thinking about policy so that policy work can be done differently—so that a deconstructive approach to policy can become part of the policy process. As Davies observes (Davies 1994: 26-28; see also Davies et al. 2006), identifying hegemonic discourses goes some way towards disrupting them. Disrupting the dominant ways in which policy and the policy realm are understood and talked about, creates space for other ways of understanding and performing policy work.

I propose that understanding both the policy realm and policies as discursively constructed can create space for policy work that achieves three things. First, it takes account of deeply-held shared values and social visions in the construction of policy problems. Second, it evaluates policies according to their broad discursive effects on people and social relations. Third, it understands the full impact of policy language, concerns and concepts in shaping policy proposals and outcomes. Very occasionally, the policy workers performed policy work directed at *addressing* the discursive character of policy language, concerns and concepts, indicating that other subversive discourses of the policy realm and policy-making exist and can be enacted. For example, one of the policy workers understood the language of 'disadvantage' as leaving unaddressed the 'advantaged' in society, those who benefit from the status quo, and attempted to redress this silence in her policy work:

> I just want to say that commonly the term 'disadvantage' is used without saying 'advantaged'. What we want to do is say 'advantage/disadvantage'. That we need to be looking at the 'advantaged' as well as the 'disadvantaged', in that the 'advantaged' are only 'advantaged' to carry on the same kind of inequitable, unjust society that always has been. …[T]hat divide between 'advantaged' and 'disadvantaged' in any kind of group or situation needs to be explicitly understood.
>
> …some people…only want to focus on, and they do focus on, a 'disadvantaged' group, but it's looking at fixing them up, it's looking at the deficit group.

This policy worker was pointing out the silences in particular policy constructions of 'disadvantage', such as a lack of attention to the ways in which some people benefit from current social and economic arrangements. She also highlighted the ways in which some people became problematic or 'the deficit group'. Rather than asserting what the 'real' problem was, as sometimes happened when the policy workers identified silences accompanying particular policy focuses, this policy worker attempted to draw attention to the *work* done by a particular policy language. She drew attention to the silencing achieved by the particular construction of 'disadvantage'. Focusing on the discursive effects of language and emphasising *how* these consequences are achieved creates space to disrupt the ways in which an issue is understood.

I wish to conclude by providing a detailed example of one type of policy work produced by the assumption of the rational and agential policy-maker. As indicated above, the policy workers' assumption that policies solve problems led them to presume that the success of a policy in solving particular policy problems could easily be judged through measuring the practical consequences of the policy against the stated objectives or desired 'outcomes'. The focus on 'outcomes' was about guiding the accurate implementation of policy objectives. For example, one of the policy workers described the 'clear government shift' to a focus on 'outcomes' as important because it allowed for greater change, or better implementation, by holding people 'accountable':

> all of education is about outcomes rather than inputs [now]. …And so the social justice action plan was about *setting targets* and reporting on how you meet your own targets. So that was much more *a focus on outcomes whereas in the past people used to talk about what they had done but there would be no change so this was meant to be holding people accountable*…Whereas a huge amount of time in the education of girls is spent on awareness-raising, you know, raising people's awareness that wasn't necessarily linked to *being able to report any discernable change that was held by any discernable data*. So I think the social justice action plan did that. (Emphasis added)

This worker's emphasis was on the need to report change, evidenced by data or specified targets. I suggest this approach reduces the effects of policies to practical measurable outcomes, eschewing the discursive frameworks in which these practical outcomes occur. Furthermore, understanding policy-as-discourse, as I espouse, includes attention to policy effects that are difficult to measure, such as the subjectivities and social relations that policies create.

Furthermore, a focus on measurable 'outcomes', captured through targets, benchmarks and indicators, restricts policies that envisage whole new ways of being and are antithetical to numerically measured 'outcomes'. For instance, when talking about policy focuses generally, a different policy worker indicated that an emphasis on the measurability of policy 'outcomes' made it difficult to justify a policy concern on the 'construction of gender':

> The focus for gender construction was great because that meant we could bring in… talking about notions of gender and young women and young men together, you know, working together for a future. It was really useful for that…and so we did a lot of stuff with future in regards to…what kind of future do we want…So I think it's much more playful, much more meaningful, but it's harder for people to grapple [with] because… you can't grab it and hold, you can't go 'well I want this many girls to be engineers'. You can't do that to it. You've got to go, 'well…I want the engineers to be…flowing gender performers'. You know [dismissive sound]. It's not as easy for people to…get their heads around. That was easy [indicating equal opportunity on a list] really. It's kind of like numbers.

This policy worker's reference to the policy focus on the 'construction of gender' creating space for discussions for the future was a rare example of the kind of policy-as-discourse approach, and the associated understanding of the discursive effects of policies, that I advocate. It suggests that such an approach to policy is possible and indicates the extent of the challenge and change I envisage. My approach, like Bacchi's, demands a focus, not so much on measurable outcomes, or on evaluating policies for their ability to 'solve' problems, but more on what kind of world, what subject positions, what silences, what categories of people, what authority, what norms of practice, what social relations and what ethics these policies create (Marginson 1997: 224-25; Ball 1994: 22; Bacchi 1999: 45; Popkewitz and Lindblad 2000; Popkewitz 1998: 1; Edelman 1988; Yeatman 1990: 158). Recognising the ways in which policy workers are located subjects within the discursive policy realm creates space to challenge traditional ways of understanding and making policy and renders possible these alternative, innovative and exciting ways of doing policy work.

References

Bacchi, C. L. (1999) *Women, Policy and Politics: The construction of policy problems.* London: Sage.
—— (2004) 'Policy and Discourse: Challenging the construction of affirmative action as preferential treatment', *Journal of European Public Policy*, 11 (1): 128-146.
Bacchi, C .L. and C. Beasley (2005) 'Reproductive Technology and the Political Limits of Care', in M. Shildrick and R. Mytikiuk (eds) *Ethics of the Body: Postconventional*

challenges, Cambridge, Massachusetts: MIT Press: 175-194.

Ball, S. J. (1990) *Politics and Policy Making in Education: Explorations in policy sociology*, London: Routledge.

—— (1993) 'What is Policy? Texts, trajectories and toolboxes', *Discourses*, 13 (2): 10-17.

—— (1994), *Education Reform: A critical and post-structural approach*, Buckingham: Open University Press.

—— (2003) 'The Teacher's Soul and the Terrors of Performativity', *Journal of Educational Policy*, 18 (2): 215-228.

Bessant, J., R. Watts, T. Dalton and P. Smyth (2006) *Talking Policy: How social policy is made*, Crows Nest: Allen and Unwin.

Bowe, R., S. J. Ball and A. Gold (1992) *Reforming Education and Changing Schools: Case studies in policy sociology*, London: Routledge.

Brown, W. (1995) *States of Injury: Power and freedom in late modernity*, Princeton, New Jersey: Princeton University Press.

Burr, V. (2003) *Social Constructionism* (2nd edition) East Sussex and New York: Routledge.

Butler, J. (1999) *Gender Trouble: Feminism and the subversion of identity*, New York: Routledge.

Davies, B. (1991) 'The Concept of Agency: A feminist poststructuralist analysis', *Social Analysis*, 30: 42-53.

—— (1994) *Poststructuralist Theory and Classroom Practice*, Geelong, Victoria: Deakin University.

Davies, B., J. Browne, S. Gannon, L. Hopkins, H. McCann and M. Wihlborg (2006) 'Constituting the Feminist Subject in Poststructuralist Discourse', *Feminism and Psychology*, 16 (1): 87-103.

Edelman, M. (1988) *Constructing the Political Spectacle*, Chicago: University of Chicago Press.

Eisenstein, H. (1996) *Inside Agitators: Australian Femocrats and the state*, Philadelphia: Temple University Press.

Eveline, J. (1994) 'The Politics of Advantage', *Australian Feminist Studies*, 19: 129-154.

Franzway, S., D. Court and R. W. Connell (1989) *Staking a Claim: Feminism, bureaucracy and the state*, Sydney: Allen and Unwin.

Gatens, M. (1998a) 'Modern Rationalism' in A. M. Jaggar and I. M. Young (eds) *A Companion to Feminist Philosophy* [ebook], Blackwell Publishers Available HTTP: <www.netlibrary.com/reader/> (accessed June 2006) 21-29.

—— (1998b) 'Institutions, Embodiment and Sexual Difference', in M. Gatens and A. Mackinnon (eds) *Gender and Institutions: Welfare, work and citizenship*, Cambridge: Cambridge University Press.

Gilbert, P. (1996) *Talking About Gender: Terminology used in the education of girls policy area and implications for policy priorities and programs*, A Women's Employment, Education and Training Advisory Group Project, Commonwealth of Australia.

Gill, Z. (2005) 'Boys: Getting it right: The "new" disadvantaged or "disadvantage" redefined?' *The Australian Educational Researcher*, 32 (2): 105-124.

Hayes, D. and B. Lingard (2003) 'Introduction: Rearticulating gender agendas in schooling: an Australian perspective', *International Journal of Inclusive Education*, 7 (1): 1-6.

Hill, H. C. (2003) 'Understanding Implementation: Street-level bureaucrats' resources for reform', *Journal of Public Administration Research and Theory*, 13 (3): 265-282.

Kenway, J. (1990) 'Gender Justice? Feminism, state theory and educational change', *Discourse*, 11 (1): 55-76.

Kingdon, J. (2003) *Agendas, Alternatives and Public Policies* (2nd edition) New York: Longman.

Lipsky, M. (1980) *Street-Level Bureaucracy: Dilemmas of the individual in public services*, New York: Russell Sage Foundation.

Lloyd, G. (1984) *The Man of Reason: 'Male' and 'female' in Western Philosophy*, London: Methuen.

Mackenzie, C. and N. Stoljar (2000) 'Introduction: Autonomy refigured', C. Mackenzie and N. Stoljar (eds) *Relational Autonomy: Feminist perspectives on autonomy, agency, and the social self*, New York: Oxford University Press.

Maclure, M. (2006) 'Entertaining Doubts: On frivolity as resistance', Education and Social Research Institute, Manchester Metropolitan University. Available HTTP: <http://www.esri.mmu.ac.uk/> (accessed November 2006).

Malloy, J. (2003) *Between Colliding Worlds: The ambiguous existence of government agencies for Aboriginal and women's policy*, Toronto: University of Toronto Press, London: Buffalo.

Marginson, S. (1997) 'Subjects and Subjugation: The economics of education as power-knowledge', *Discourse: studies in the cultural politics of education*, 18 (2): 215-227.

Patai, D. and N. Koertge (1994) *Professing Feminism: Cautionary tales from the strange world of Women's Studies*, New York: Basic Books.

Popkewitz, T. S. (1996) 'Rethinking Decentralization and the State/Civil Society Distinctions: The state as a problematic of governing', *Journal of Education Policy*, 11 (1): 27-51.

—— (1998) 'The Culture of Redemption and the Administration of Freedom as Research', *Review of Educational Research*, 68 (1): 1-34.

Popkewitz, T. and S. Lindblad (2000) 'Educational Governance and Social Inclusion and Exclusion: Some conceptual difficulties and problematics in policy and research', *Discourse: studies in the cultural politics of education*, 21 (1): 5-44.

Pringle, R. and S. Watson (1992) '"Women's Interests" and the Post-Structuralist State' in M. Barrett and A. Phillips (eds) *Destabilizing Theory: Contemporary feminist debates*, Cambridge: Polity Press, 53-73.

Rothfield, P. (1992) 'Thinking Embodiment, Practicing the Body: Medical ethics, Foucault and feminism', *Meridian*, 11 (2): 37-47.

Shore, C. and S. Wright (1997) 'Policy: A new field of anthropology', C. Shore and S. Wright (eds) *Anthropology of Policy: Critical perspectives on governance and power*, London and New York: Routledge, 3-39.

Taylor, S. (1997) 'Critical Policy Analysis: Exploring contexts, texts and consequences', *Discourse: studies in the cultural politics of education*, 18 (1): 23-35.

—— (2004) 'Researching Educational Policy and Change in "New Times": Using critical discourse analysis', *Journal of Education Policy*, 19 (4): 433-451.

Taylor, S., F. Rizvi, B. Lingard and M. Henry (1997) *Educational Policy and the Politics of Change*, New York: Routledge.

Watts, R. (1993/94) 'Government and Modernity: An essay in thinking Governmentality', *Arena Journal*, 2: 103-157.

Yeatman, A. (1990) *Bureaucrats, Technocrats, Femocrats: Essays on the contemporary Australian State*, Sydney: Allen and Unwin.

—— (ed.) (1998a) *Activism and the Policy Process*, St Leonards, NSW: Allen and Unwin.

—— (ed.) (1998b) 'Introduction' and 'Activism and the policy process', *Activism and the Policy Process*, St Leonards, NSW: Allen and Unwin, 1-35.

Yates, L. (1993) *The Education of Girls: Policy, research and the question of gender*, Victoria: Australian Council Educational Research.

—— (1996) 'Who Are Girls and What Are We Trying To Do To Them in Schools? Changing assumptions and visions in contemporary education reforms', *School Days: Past, present and future. Education of Girls in 20th Century Australia*, an edited collection of papers from the Conference held at Magill Campus, University of South Australia, 20-21 September 1996. University of South Australia: Research Centre for Gender Studies and the Faculty of Education, 3-10.

Additional interventions: Select reading list

Begley, A. and J. Coveney (2010) 'Wonder Vitamin or Mass Medication? Media and academic representation of folate fortification as a policy problem in Australia and New Zealand', *Australian and New Zealand Journal of Public Health*, 34 (5): 466-471.

Carson, L. and K. Edwards (2011) 'Prostitution and Sex Trafficking: What are the problems represented to be? A discursive analysis of law and policy in Sweden and Victoria, Australia', *Australian Feminist Law Journal*, 34: 63-87.

Cort, P. (2010a) 'Stating the Obvious: The European Qualifications Framework is not a neutral evidence-based policy tool', *European Educational Research Journal*, 9 (3): 304-316.

—— (2010b) 'Europeanisation and Policy Change in the Danish Vocational Education and Training System', *Research in Comparative and International Education*, 5 (3): 331-343.

Coveney, J. (2010) 'Analyzing Public Health Policy: Three approaches', *Health Promotion Practice*, 11 (4): 515-521.

Crocco, M. (2006) 'Gender and Social Education: What's the problem?', in E. Wayne Ross (ed.) *The Social Studies Curriculum: Purposes, problems, and possibilities*. (3rd Edition). New York: State University of New York Press, 171-196.

Edwards, J. (2003) 'The Policy Panoptic of "Mutual Obligations"', *Journal of Educational Enquiry*, 4 (1): 97-116.

Edwards, K. (2010) 'Social Inclusion: Is this a way forward for young people and should we go there?', *Youth Studies Australia*, 29 (2): 16-24.

Eggebø, H. (2010) 'The Problem of Dependency: Immigration, gender, and the Welfare State', *Social Politics: International Studies in Gender, State and Society*, 17 (3): 295-322.

El-murr, A. (2010) 'Representing the Problem of Abortion: Language and the Policy Making process in the Abortion Law Reform Project in Victoria, 2008', *The Australian Feminist*

Law Journal, 33: 121-140.

Fraser, S. and D. Moore (2011) 'Governing through problems: The formulation of policy on amphetamine-type stimulants (ATS) in Australia', *International Journal of Drug Policy*, 22: 498-506.

Goodwin, S. (2011) 'Analysing Policy as Discourse: Methodological advances in policy analysis', in L. Markauskaite, P. Freebody and J. Irwin (eds) *Methodological Choice and Design: Scholarship, policy and practice in social and educational research*. Dordrecht: Springer, 167-180.

Gordon, Z. (2011) 'Deconstructing "Aboriginal Welfare Dependency": Using postcolonial theory to reorientate Indigenous Affairs', *Journal of Australian Indigenous Issues*, 14 (2-3): 14-29.

Hutchinson, J. and J. Eveline (2010) 'Workplace Bullying Policy in the Australian Public Sector: Why has gender been ignored?', *Australian Journal of Public Administration*, 69 (1): 47-60.

Krook, M. L. and S. Childs (eds) (2010) *Women, Gender, and Politics: A reader*, New York: Oxford University Press.

Lister, R. (2010) *Understanding Theories and Concepts in Social Policy*, Bristol: Policy Press.

Maddox, M. (2001) *For God and Country: Religious dynamics in Australian federal politics*. Canberra: Department of the Parliamentary Library.

Meier, P., E. Lombardo and M. Bustello (2005) 'Gender Mainstreaming and the Benchmarking Fallacy of Women in Political Decision Making', *The Greek Review of Social Research*, 117: 35-61.

Murray, S. and A. Powell (2009) 'What's the Problem?: Australian public policy constructions of domestic and family violence', *Violence Against Women*, 15 (5): 532-552.

Paterson, S. (2010) 'What's the problem with gender-based analysis? Gender mainstreaming policy and practice in Canada,' *Canadian Public Administration*, 53 (3): 395-416.

Powell, A. and S. Murray (2008) 'Children and Domestic Violence: Constructing a policy problem in Australia and New Zealand', *Social and Legal Studies*, 17 (4): 453-473.

Saari, M. (2011) 'Promoting Gender Equality Without a Gender Perspective: Problem representations of equal pay in Finland', *Gender, Work and Organization*, Early View, Article first published online, 13 April. Available via HTTP: <http://onlinelibrary.wiley.com/doi/10.1111/j.1468-0432.2011.00554.x/pdf>

Shaw, S. (2010) 'Reaching the Parts that Other Theories and Methods Can't Reach: How and why a policy-as-discourse approach can inform health-related policy', *Health*, 14 (2): 196-212.

Spanger, M. (2011) 'Human Trafficking as Lever for Feminist Voices? Transformations of the Danish policy field of prostitution', *Critical Social Policy*, 31 (4): 517-539.

Stenvoll, D. (2002) 'From Russia with Love? Newspaper coverage of cross-border prostitution in Northern Norway, 1990-2001', *European Journal of Women's Studies*, 9 (2): 143-162.

Widding, U. (2011) 'Problematic parents and the community parent education: Representations of social class, ethnicity, and gender', *Journal of Feminist Family Therapy*, 23 (1): 19-38.

Part III

Strategic exchanges: The wider context

8 | Making politics fleshly: The ethic of social flesh

CHRIS BEASLEY AND CAROL BACCHI[1]

Introduction

In this chapter we (Chris and Carol) consider the genesis of the concept of 'social flesh', our imaginative reconceptualisation of social space and social relations. This concept emerged from a close working partnership over several years and from a series of joint publications. Here we trace the stages in the development of our ideas, moving specifically from queries about the disjunction between theories of citizenship and embodiment to exploration of how the concept 'social flesh' produces new ways of thinking about a range of pressing contemporary political issues. Specifically we offer the concept as a counter to the currently hegemonic ethic of neo-liberal 'man'.

We aim to articulate explicitly our conceptual trajectory, outlining in a step by step fashion how we developed the notion of social flesh. The chapter provides a chronological and accretive account of the way in which we moved, partially in response to personal experiences, through a series of literatures consequent upon our concern to challenge the neo-liberal (presumptive masculine) 'individual'. In the process of outlining this trajectory, we discuss the difficulties we found in the scholarship associated respectively with mainstream and feminist writings on citizenship, literature attending to community and social interconnection including those referring to trust and care, the body of work dealing with democratic theory, and finally analytical materials focussed upon social movements and socio-political change. This sequential critique of existing literatures works towards the assembling of a constructive alternative framework. Moreover, the identification of factors—involving intersecting

---

[1] Carol Bacchi would like to acknowledge the research assistance of Anne Wilson.

personal, emotional, bodily, intellectual and professional elements—which shaped this conceptual trajectory, also provides a contribution to an ethnography of research practices.

The formation of 'social flesh'

Part of the story of 'social flesh' is how we came to work together. And an important element of that story is our shared experience of mothering and our attempts to 'fit' mothering together with paid labour. The significance of mothering was no doubt highlighted for us because we both faced particular 'challenges' in our experience of it. Stephen—Carol's son—(and Carol) developed a feeding disorder at (his) age of eight weeks. We say 'and Carol' because, the narrative/memoir (*Fear of Food* 2003), which describes this time in their lives, explores the lingering confusion in Carol's mind about the extent to which her son was 'really' sick and the extent to which her need for order and predictability in her life exacerbated the

Fear of Food **book cover.**

Perry, Chris, and medical staff, *The Sunday Mail* 16 July 1995, p. 28.

'problem'. Chris's daughter, Perry, was born very prematurely at around six months gestation and remained in hospital for five months. Perry (and Chris) lived with an oxygen mask and cylinder, as well as a rigorous drug regime, for a further number of months once Perry was physically able to leave the hospital.

Chris visited Carol in Canberra before Perry was born and while Carol was coping with the feeding 'problem'. We became friends, friends who supported each other as best we could through the continuing challenges of trying to fit together 'good enough' mothering and 'good enough' academic pursuits. We often spoke of the specific difficulties we faced and tried to devise strategies to improve the 'fit' between our 'domestic' and 'public' lives. These 'practical' discussions turned into theory. Specifically we began to ask why and how our embodied experiences of mothering did not count for anything in our 'other' lives—why and how our mothering was invisible, or supposed to be invisible, when it was so important—not only to us and our immediate contacts but to the wider society. Put slightly differently, we asked why our embodied experience of mothering did not register as part of our role as political subjects who are called 'citizens'.

The term 'citizen bodies' came to capture the character of our initial questions. This phrase appears in the titles of the first two articles related to 'social flesh' (Beasley and Bacchi 2000; Bacchi and Beasley 2002) that we produced, three of eventually five journal articles (Bacchi and Beasley 2005b; Beasley and Bacchi 2005, 2007), one book chapter (Bacchi and Beasley 2005a) and a conference paper (Bacchi and Beasley 2004) thus far. The second article (published in *Critical Social Policy* in 2002) asked pointedly: 'Is embodied citizenship a contradiction in terms?'

Before explaining how we went about addressing this question, it is important to say something about our (embodied) working methods. We initiated a practice in which we alternated as primary authors. We recognised that this was the only way we would ever find the time to see our project/s to completion, and that (incidentally) it would increase our publication 'output'. We met when and how we could to thrash out ideas. Once we met in a rented holiday cabin in Victor Harbor, a beachside town in South Australia, where we were trying to give our kids a holiday. Once we met in a cafe when we managed to snatch a couple of hours from our compressed life/work regime. Mostly, however, we met at each other's houses in snatched moments between our many waged work and domestic tasks. Wherever the meeting, we taped the exchanges on a small dictaphone and later Carol typed them up. These notes, which moved through a free flow of ideas towards a structure, became the basis of the specific article that emerged. (However, in writing this chapter, for the first time, we each wrote specific sections of the chapter separately from the start.)

In this intellectual partnership we used each other as resources. At first glance we made a rather odd couple. We came from very different disciplinary backgrounds—Carol from History/Politics, Chris from an interdisciplinary background including Cultural Studies and Sociology. We had different feminist backgrounds as well. Carol's feminist perspective arose out a form of liberal feminism, whereas Chris' stance arose from socialist/radical feminism. Perhaps most significantly, we had different working styles, partly due to our training, partly due to our personalities. Carol may be characterised by her steady, thorough, 'nit-picking' approach, while Chris's mode might be viewed more in terms of an impetuous, enthusiastic effervescence. The marked difference in styles could be characterised as a contrast between a 'slow burn' (Carol) and the sharp flare of a light bulb (Chris). What eventuated from our collaboration came through a working from and out of such differences, and involved a continuous moving back and forth, a testing, seeking ways to illuminate the lives we found ourselves leading. Carol's asceticism tempered Chris's hedonism. Chris's passion countered Carol's reticence. It seemed that an unlikely combination could, after all, be highly productive.

We brought this ongoing dialogue, as noted, to the term 'citizen bodies', as our starting place for thinking through what we felt was amiss or lacking in existing literatures on the topics of citizenship and embodiment. We asked what happens to theorising around social subjects if these two terms, so often kept at a distance, are interlaced together—as we felt they must be. We were very well aware of the perils involved in adopting the language of citizenship because of the ways it conventionally evokes nation-state schematics. All the same we adopted the term as a base-line for re-imagining more inclusive forms of sociality.

Looking first at mainstream and feminist literature on citizenship, we detected that bodies, when they appeared (which was not often), did so in very specific and delimited ways. Specifically we found that bodies were treated in an instrumental fashion, as something people 'had' and 'owned' and 'controlled'. The languages of 'bodily integrity' and 'autonomy', for example, featured largely in feminist reflections on issues like rape and abortion. We saw the usefulness of those languages, particularly in making certain kinds of political claims, but mused on what they left out. The model of subjectivity underpinning these approaches to bodies seemed to us to oddly mimic a mind (controlling) body dichotomy that feminists had long found inadequate and troubling. On this basis we asked, do people really consider and treat their bodies as something they can and want to control on a day-to-day basis? If 'control' is a major way of articulating our relationship 'with' our bodies (without even considering the puzzle of just exactly what this control could mean), what difference would it make to a range of political issues to rethink this 'relationship'? Where, we speculated, was 'flesh'—our inescapably fleshly materiality? In brief, we found existing citizenship literature oddly disembodied.

In this context, we also noted how mainstream (and much feminist) citizenship theory equated citizenship with 'public sphere' activities. The issue underpinning many feminist interventions was how to reduce the barriers to public sphere participation that women faced. In these analyses women's 'private' associations constituted a barrier to participation in the public sphere and hence to full citizenship. While recognising the importance of public participation, we asked what could be achieved by reconceptualising an association with the 'private' as a *resource* rather than as a *limitation*, imagining how such a conceptual shift might be suggestive of alternative notions of political sociality. To clarify, by 'resource' we mean a strategic political intervention, not an epistemological foundation.

Our concern with the disembodied and public conceptualisation of citizenship led us to turn to body theory, and specifically to feminist body theory. Here we focused on scholars such as Elizabeth Grosz (1987, 1994, 1996) and found much to embrace, specifically the attempt to reconfigure the nature of the subject/body 'relationship'. Grosz's exemplification of this 'relationship' is expressed in the image of the mobius strip where there is no fixed 'inside' or 'outside' to our embodied experiences. Bodies in Grosz's account are neither consistently 'other' than minds/selves/subjects nor consistently at one with them. There is no stable mind/body split or unity. Despite the redolent character of such reflections, we nevertheless found that they tended to be highly abstracted and oddly individualistic, focusing on a *particular* bodily subject (Beasley and Bacchi 2000). The subsequent neglect of *inter*-subject relations reduced, in our view, the political usefulness of such theory. Where, we wondered, was the 'social' in these fleshly imaginings?

We found Sarah Ahmed's (1998, 1999) focus on how subjects are constituted by the manner in which they are touched particularly evocative. Carol Johnson's (2002) analysis of heteronormativity and touch offered another important contribution to the analysis of embodied subjectivity, as did studies of breastfeeding mothers (Stearns 1999; Reiger 1999; Bartlett 2000) and of persons with disabilities (Seymour 1998; Meekosha and Dowse 1997).

In our search for 'citizen bodies', in other words, we found 'social flesh'. Citizenship theory, we concluded, needed some *flesh* on its bones while body theory needed to become more *social*.

The material of social flesh

Though there are important debates in mainstream and particularly feminist literature on citizenship about the meaning of community and thus the positioning of subjects within the social, such discussions did not apparently enable a thoroughly embodied understanding of sociality and social interconnection between subjects (Beasley and Bacchi 2000). Yet, it seemed to us, that developing ways of registering, appreciating and deploying awareness of the fleshly social were of increasingly urgent significance.

In our contemporary world we have seen the rise and rise of dominant neo-liberal understandings of sociality as matters of individual choice and 'rational' (read self-interested, cognitive) decision-making. However, at the same time, throughout the world the terrible bodily assaults of violence, suffering and poverty continue, while human beings also find themselves in an ever more fragile physical environment. Mitchell Dean has made the point that neo-liberalism is an ethos (Dean 1997 in Larner 2002: 19). For us, this highlighted the need to put forward a *contesting* political ethic. That said, we had some significant reservations about the capacities of the commonly employed alternative approaches—signalled by terms like trust, respect, care, responsibility, etc.—to achieve this goal. It is in this context that we developed an 'other' concept, the ethic of social flesh.

'Trust' and 'care' are the most widely endorsed vocabularies for offering a shared challenge to the neo-liberal ethos of atomistic individualism and the accompanying problems of attending to social interconnection/community. 'Trust' engages scholars, social commentators, and politicians alike as the 'goanna oil' solution to our troubles. Trust enthusiasts in the main see excessive individualisation as a threat to social cohesion and responsible citizen behaviour (Putnam 2000; Fukuyama 1995). By contrast, those who talk about 'care', including feminist, welfare-oriented and postmodern thinkers, largely come from a different perspective, with a primary focus upon the need to develop humane, tolerant social relations (e.g. Tronto 2001; Sevenhuijsen 2003; Kittay 1998; Bauman 1993). Associated languages align with either trust or care. For example, 'respect' aligns with trust, while 'responsibility' and 'generosity' align with care, though the vocabularies are by no means entirely separate. The crucial point here is that, despite the widespread support for languages like trust and care, we saw significant problems with these as alternatives to the political ethos of neo-liberalism (Beasley and Bacchi 2007, 2005; Bacchi and Beasley 2002).

Firstly, in both terms (trust and care) there is an insufficient attention to embodiment. Trust—and connected terms like respect—for the most part simply fail to attend to bodies, such that the emphasis is on reform of what appears as cognitive functioning (Bacchi and Beasley 2004, 2005b). Care ethicists, however, do put embodiment on the socio-political agenda, whether they focus upon micro one-to-one caring relationships or care as a macro social practice with institutional and governance implications. All the same, even care ethicists deal only with quite specific aspects of embodiment—typically those to do with bodily maintenance and nurturance, such as elder and child care. Alternative conceptions of ethical community require, in our view, a more expansive understanding of embodied intersubjectivity. We wish precisely to look for a more substantive way of gripping together the corporeal and the socio-political—of grasping simultaneously the sociality of flesh and the physicality of social life.

Secondly, both trust and care offer an insufficient challenge to liberal individualism. This is particularly evident in relation to our concern with embodiment. Trust and care are frequently concerned with improving citizens. Indeed, both tend to emphasise the need to improve citizen's *moral* attributes, which returns us to a rather individualised, cognitive actor, and often to a highly prescriptive understanding of individual virtues as the basis of socio-political change. This ignores problematic elements of simply endorsing forms of altruism like trust and care within *already hierarchical* societies, which brings us to the third critique.

Thirdly, the languages of trust and care provide an insufficiently critical approach to the virtue of altruism. Trust thinkers, despite promoting a more altruistic community, are inclined to reinstate social hierarchies between the 'less fortunate' and the 'more privileged' (Bacchi and Beasley 2005b). The socio-political change that is envisaged appears more as an erratum to enable the smoother, less harsh functioning of a neo-liberal competitive hierarchical society. The rich are to remain as rich as ever, but learn to be nicer about it. Care ethicists generally offer a more challenging commentary in this respect, given their concern to support caring at micro and macro levels. However—in spite of care ethicists' expressed desires to avoid paternalism—an asymmetrical relationship is constructed between those *needing* care and those *delivering* care, which we feel undermines the egalitarian potential of the analysis.

This distinction between the needy (the vulnerable), and those attending to their needs (the 'generous' or beneficent), also marks those post-structuralist-postmodern thinkers who ground a new ethical sociality around 'care'. The work of Emmanuel Levinas is influential here, shaping a number of contemporary writings concerned with *care for the 'other'*—including, for instance, work by Jacques Derrida, Julia Kristeva, Iris Marion Young, Margrit Shildrick, Ros Diprose, and Anthony Burke, among others. While Levinas (1998) does not use the word 'care', his focus upon 'responsibility', on compassion for the 'other', replicates the compassionate action of care ethics. Hence, in trust, care, and responsibility, in all these accounts, the caring 'exchange' is viewed consistently as a form of altruism—that is, as one side giving to the 'other' side (Beasley and Bacchi 2007).

One might say in this context, 'what's the problem with altruism?' Surely altruism is a good and wonderful thing. The difficulty here in our view is that once again there is a turn towards promoting the assumed presently deficient virtue of *individual* citizens. More than this, establishing altruism as the *starting point* for reform of society neglects or understates the connections between altruism and power, and reinstates hierarchical relations between groups of people that precisely undermine development of new egalitarian social relations. A political ethic based on altruism becomes limited to protecting 'the weak' by establishing minimum conditions or rights—a reformist political agenda that does not encourage a reimagining of

Spencer Tunick - Mexico City installation.

social interconnection (Bacchi and Beasley 2005b). Paternalist protectionism is only a partial challenge to neo-liberal thinking.

To be sure, the vocabulary of care does at least acknowledge that all of us are physically vulnerable and need care. However, by contrast, we wish to stress not our 'shared vulnerability' but *embodied co-existence*. The terminology of 'social flesh' involves a refusal of what we see as the residues of 'noblesse oblige' that still seem to linger in continuing emphasis upon needy vulnerability and extending altruism (Beasley and Bacchi 2007). By contrast, social flesh highlights human embodied interdependence. We found the evocative possibilities of such a perspective registered, for instance, in Spencer Tunick's Mexico City art installation of an expanse of naked people linked by joined arms. By drawing attention to shared embodied reliance, mutual reliance, of people across the globe on social space, infrastructure and resources, the perspective of social flesh offers a decided challenge to neo-liberal conceptions of the autonomous self and at the same time removes the supposedly already given distinction between 'strong' and 'weak'.

Social flesh is thus a strategic conceptual intervention—a point that will shortly be clarified further—which has significant implications for democratic visions. The political vocabulary of social flesh puts forward both an ontological perspective and contingent political directions. We agree with care ethicists that sociality *is* embodied, that embodied interconnection is the pre-existing condition of human life and therefore of sociality. However, what human beings do with this ontological state of interconnection is always political. The questions in this context are, what political vision/s might social flesh invoke (how might we rethink sociality)? And secondly what is to be done to move towards a recognition of social flesh? Thus the conceptual intervention of social flesh is both about 'what *is*' and 'what *might be*'. It is both a thin ontological starting point and a realm of political possibilities within particular forms of sociality, including a mode of political imaginary or utopian ideal which acts as a counter-foil to the self-evident 'natural' status of dominant neo-liberal political understandings and practices.

The issue from our point of view is what does this terminology enable? What can you do with it? We will attend to this issue first of all by providing an illustration of how the concept might be employed in the setting of Australian politics. This illustration will then be followed by reference to a second example which is focussed upon sexuality and leads to a concluding note.

Politics and social flesh

'Social flesh', as argued in the previous section, is offered as a 're-vision', as an ethico-political starting point for thinking critically about politics, interconnection and sociality. Ways of thinking social relationships have political significance and consequences. To illustrate this proposition, this section of the chapter explores the differences which recognition of social flesh could make to the theory and practice of democratic politics in Australia. In order to consider this application of the ethic of social flesh, we initially look at the range of existing theoretical approaches to understanding democracy and their comparative limits with regard to their grasp of embodied sociality, and after that turn to a practical indicative application.

In mainstream democratic theory unsurprisingly we find the same rational, disembodied subject that we had identified as hegemonic in much citizenship literature, as discussed earlier (Beasley and Bacchi 2000). This insight is hardly new. Indeed, feminist scholars (such as Pateman 1983) have made this point for some time. Hence, we turned our attention to theoretical contributions from the broadly characterised 'left' of the political spectrum.

'Left' contributions to democratic theory can be organised roughly into two camps, those primarily concerned with establishing forms of *consensus* as a necessary grounding for democratic organization, and those who insist that democracies must attend to '*difference*', with overlap at times between these groups. Among the former we would place Jürgen Habermas and deliberative democrats. Among the latter we would find some feminists (for instance Young 1990), some postcolonial theorists (including Said 1979) and 'radical democracy' advocates (such as Mouffe 2002; Laclau 1990; Connolly 1993, 1995). 'Consensus' theorists tend to emphasize the importance of rational debate within democracies. For Habermas (1979, 1990, 1996), a public sphere of rational debate is the only possible foundation for democratic politics. Deliberative democrats, following Habermas, focus heavily on 'communicative exchanges' and on developing citizens' rhetorical and interpretive 'capacities'. As one example, Frank Fischer's (2003: 236) declared objective is to 'create spaces for democratic participation that offer a place for reason in both goal-setting and conflict management'. The focus on reason and reasoned debate means that bodies simply do not appear, as both Iris Marion Young (1990: 125) and William Connolly (1995: 13) have noted.

'Difference' democrats score a little better on this question. Feminist theorists, including Carole Pateman (1988), Iris Marion Young (1989, 1990) and Toril Moi (1999), have important things to say about the 'lived body' and 'differentiated citizenship' (see discussion in Bacchi and Eveline 2010: 94-95). However, this attention to embodiment in 'difference' models of democracy remains rather under-developed and is unevenly present. For example, radical democrats Chantal Mouffe (1992: 381) and Ernesto Laclau (1990: 184) express concerns about the essentialist assumptions underpinning perspectives like these and, on the assumption that recognition of bodies necessarily equates to biologism, offer *in its place* a focus on how 'the subject is constructed through different discourses and subject positions'. Mouffe (2002) overtly critiques the rational/reasoning agent pursued by deliberative theorists, but does not engage in any depth with 'the body'. Despite occasional references to the 'concrete' and to 'one's materiality', Laclau (1990: 184) also has little to say about bodies. Indeed, with the exception of Connolly's (1995: 194-95) suggestive reference to the 'corporealization of culture', the most widely employed 'difference' model—radical democracy—says nothing about bodies. Putting 'social flesh' into democratic theory, we argue, fills this lacuna.

To illustrate its potential, we reflect on the history of and debate engendered by the 'strangers in the house' incidents in Australia. These incidents involved the expulsion of breast-feeding mothers and children from the Australian state and federal Houses of Parliament. Considering the arguments engendered by these incidents allows us to rethink relations between 'private' and 'public', specifically considering how reconceptualising an association with the 'private' as a *resource* rather than as a *limitation or barrier* might be suggestive of alternative notions of political sociality.

Initially there were two 'incidents' that sparked the debates raised by the presence of breast-feeding mothers and of children. On the first occasion in Victoria in 2003 MLA Kirstie Marshall, who was breastfeeding her infant son, was asked to leave the state Legislative Assembly during question time (Holland 2002-03). On the second occasion (18 June 2009) Senator Sarah Hanson-Young's two-year-old child was removed from the federal government's Senate at the request of the President (Rodriguez 2009: 1). On the first occasion the expressed reason for the expulsion was that, in accordance with formal parliamentary procedures, there is restricted access to visitors or 'strangers' to Houses of Parliament. The history of these rules, which derive from parliamentary practice in the United Kingdom, is pertinent to the discussion. According to Rodriguez (2009: 3), the practice dates back to the need to preserve

Tandberg, *The Age,* **20 June 2009.**

the secrecy of debate from the monarch. By the eighteenth century the issue was more likely to have been about 'avoiding accountability to the public'. In keeping with this rationale, the public in Britain was not permitted to visit the British House of Commons until 1845, and then only after paying a fee. This background is at least suggestive of disturbingly anti-democratic sentiments buried in the Australian parliamentary rules.

Today the reason most often defended for precluding infants/children is 'disruption'. In 2002 Betty Boothroyd, the first woman Speaker of the United Kingdom House of Commons, made the case that feeding a child during chamber and committee session was 'not in the interests of both parliamentary business and the child itself, due to likely disruptions':

> I do not believe that the feeding of babies in either the Chamber or Committee is conducive to the efficient conduct of public business. Nor do I think that the necessary calm environment in which to feed babies can be provided in such circumstances. (Boothroyd 2001: 29 in Rodriguez 2009: 15)

In Australia in 2009, Pru Goward, former federal Sex Discrimination Commissioner, made a similar case: '[y]ou can't be distracted. The chamber for a parliamentarian is like an operating theatre for a surgeon. It's where the main business is done' (quoted in Warhurst 2009: 15 in Rodriguez 2009: 2). Here the opponents of breastfeeding in Parliament are both women and in one case a woman charged with official defence of equal opportunity. Clearly the issues raised cross both gender and conventional political lines.

On the argument about disruption, there is an odd tension in Boothroyd's comments. On the one hand it is implied that the feeding of babies is itself disruptive while, on the other hand, the lack of a 'calm environment' is noted as a problem. Gillian Calvert (2009), New South Wales Commissioner for Children and Young People, pointed out the contradiction: '[t]here doesn't seem to be a problem with screaming adults in the Parliament, so I don't think that noise is the issue'.

Ambivalent reactions to breastfeeding in public extend well beyond Parliament. Often concern is expressed that men may be distracted by the activity and possible display of a woman's breast. As Alison Bartlett (2000) points out, breastfeeding puts bodies onto the agenda in no uncertain terms. Since 1995, some changes have eventuated. However, apart from the Australian Senate, only the Legislative Assembly of the Australian Capital Territory and the Legislative Council of New South Wales—that is, certain houses of state government parliaments—have allowed breastfeeding mothers and their infants into the chamber. Tellingly, it was not until 2004 that the term 'visitors' formally replaced 'strangers' in the standing orders of the Australian federal House of Representatives, though the term 'strangers' has remained within the 'informal lexicon of parliamentary practice' (Rodriguez 2009: 5-6, 10).

It is important to reflect on the terms of the debate within which these changes have occurred. Reform is generally defended on the grounds that democratic parliaments need to become more modern and to reflect changing attitudes towards 'work-life balance'. More specifically, the need for change is tied to the desirability of encouraging more women to enter political life. The Greens leader, Bob Brown, who registered a motion of dissent to the expulsion of Hansen-Young's child and who subsequently moved a change to the standing orders, put this case:

> We are in a society…in which, generally, we are parenting at an older and older age. We are also in a society in which we want to encourage parents to be part of the political process, because that is central to the democratic aims of any society. We are certainly in a society which needs to encourage more women to enter politics. (Brown 2009: 3907)

> This position fits well within current conceptions of anti-discrimination and equal opportunity. (Rodriquez 2009: 14)

These forms of argument rely upon and reinforce a view of democracy that emphasises participation, specifically women's participation. To facilitate women's access, children are to be admitted to the House in 'rare' circumstances and for 'brief periods' (Brown 2009: 3910). To improve democracy, women's needs, we are told, must be 'accommodated'. Despite qualifications to the contrary (Evans 2009: 3907), there is an assumption that children remain primarily *women's* responsibility. In Bob Brown's words, the requirements of 'mothers, and indeed fathers' might be accommodated with the proviso that 'if they bring a child in here, the child should not be disruptive, the time should be brief and it should only be done on rare occasions' (Brown 2009: 3910; see also Evans 2009: 3907). In this account the 'private' and bodies are constituted as exceptions, reinscribing the 'public' and disembodiment as normative.

This normative inscription of disembodiment may be seen again in the most recent instance concerning children in parliament—that is, the instance of Australian Labor Party member for Sydney, Tanya Plibersek, and her newborn baby, Louis. Plibersek's attendance in the federal House of Representatives is particularly important given the context in 2010 of a Labor Party minority government. In a show of understanding the Opposition agreed to neutralise one of their votes if Plibersek were unable to be present as a result of her childcare responsibilities—though this agreement applies only while she is on maternity leave. However, this new limited recognition of embodied care demands, is undercut by Plibersek's insistence that she will not breastfeed in the House and that mothering responsibilities would not 'interfere' with her parliamentary duties (in Squires 2010: 3). She judges, no doubt quite reasonably, that breastfeeding babies are still in fact 'strangers' in public spaces and that mothering remains an individual woman's 'private' concern.

Invoking social flesh, insisting upon our embodied fleshly intersubjectivity, alters the terms of these reflections and exchanges. As a strategic intervention, it renders the normative 'strange'. Hence, we end up not with 'strangers in the house' but with a 'strange house'. What, the reader may well ask, is strange about it? In this house, there are no children. What follows from their absence? The disavowal of children represents and produces a denial or blocking out of certain dimensions of human interconnection. It indicates an unwillingness to think about bodies in all their fleshy materiality. Indeed there is nothing like a crying, excreting infant to remind us of where and how we all started.

To be clear, we are *not* suggesting that children ought to be present at Parliamentary proceedings, but we *are* asking how social priorities might be re-evaluated *if they were*. Our intervention thus operates alongside of but at a different level from demands to increase children's rights (Franklin 1986; O'Neill 1992; John 1995) or to recognize children's 'voices' (Kulynych 2001). Rather we see advantages in asking the question, what would happen with 'children in the house'? What kinds of issues, for example, might take on a different emphasis? Certainly the presence of children, with all their unruly fleshliness, might lead to a rethink in industrial relations policy and the priority currently placed on work as 'the measure of man'. In foreign policy it might spark much-needed discussion of death, dismemberment and combat-related trauma as the anticipated results of war. In health policy a focus on dependents might pose a challenge to the current individualisation of health-related issues. The presence of children in the Chambers would certainly complicate claims like those of the South Australian Minister for Health, John Hill (in Kelton 2007), who has confidently asserted that '[u]p to 50 per cent of diseases are determined by lifestyle choices'. The presumption of individual control, and hence the premise of neo-liberal rationality, underpinning such discussions becomes an issue in the case of children. In what sense, one might ask, does it make sense to blame children for not taking care of their health? Parents of course become the common target in this situation. However, the presence of children provides at least one interruption in a dominant narrative about individual responsibility for health.

The evidence of 'other' bodies does, it would seem, encourage a rethinking of political priorities. For example, in the context of state government excitement about spending significant funds on a new football stadium, South Australia's first Member of Parliament with an acknowledged disability, Kelly Vincent, noted the comparative incongruity of the years that 'people wait for a wheelchair', despite the crucial importance of such facilities for simple mobility and their relatively limited cost (Orr 2010: 11).

Clearly, Parliament is not the *only* 'strange house'. Many of us currently work in 'strange houses'. As a reconceptualisation of embodied sociality, social flesh can make the familiar strange in evocative ways. As Chela Sandoval (2000: 6) explains, 'new terminologies help bring unprecedented modes of consciousness, agency, and collective action into being'. In this vein social flesh opens up new horizons by offering different models for political and social/living arrangements.

New social theorising

We have asked, what difference would recognition of social flesh make to the theory and practice of democratic politics in Australia? What does this terminology enable? We used the instance of trying to imagine the political implications of what a breasted lactating parliament might mean. To bring into focus the strategic possibilities of conceiving a political ethos of fleshly mutual interdependence, we will now briefly turn to imagining the political implications of a libidinous desiring polity—a polity of social *sexual* flesh.

On the one hand, we are all accustomed to occasional displays of naked flesh as a

Carrette, 'No War'.

socio-political strategy. We know that an unexpected flash of flesh can have the impact that Shelley attributed to poetry: 'it strips the veil of familiarity from the world' (Shelley 1821, in Douglas-Fairhurst 2011). There are many examples of this use of flesh as surprise, which enables the registering of a point. As illustrations we draw attention to just a couple of them where the revealed body is meant specifically to remind us of our shared interconnected location as physical creatures: one, an anti-war protest of exposed bodies in Sydney in 2003 in which the naked bodies are arranged to themselves spell out 'NO WAR' and the second a political declaration regarding ethical treatment of other animals' bodies.

Yet despite this occasional usage of nakedness, of unveiled embodiment as political strategy, most often such usages are precisely desexualised, in keeping with our culture's tendency to regard the sexual body as perhaps the most private of private matters—as highly personal, shameful or even disgusting—the *sexual* body is barely present in political thought or action. Indeed any social—that is, any group or mass—presentation of the sexual body seems hardly imaginable as politics. In this setting, it is remarkably difficult to find a way to express the *libidinous* character of the political ethic of social flesh.

Spencer Tunick's living artworks usefully come to our aide once again here in conjuring an evocative representation of how we might express sociality as libidinal flesh. Tunick's Sydney Opera House 2010 art installation provides a vista of mass nude hugging, with many people embracing strangers, which—despite the limits of its couple and largely white-skinned orientation—perhaps goes toward capturing the vital meaning of social flesh as shared, interconnected, sexual/intimate physicality. This political imaginary brings to the fore the strangeness of the social, when its sensual fleshliness is unveiled, and offers us a different

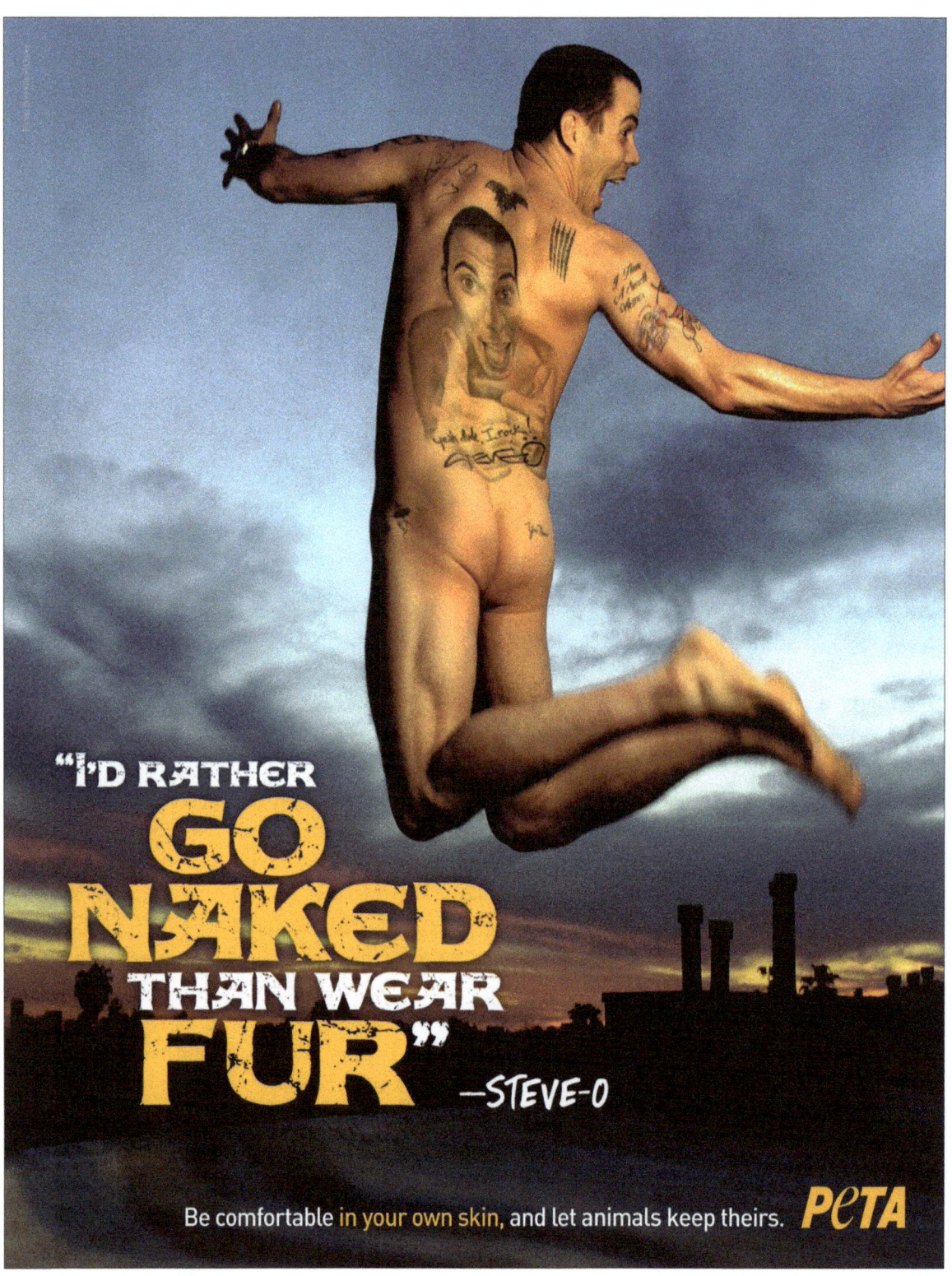

PETA poster.

perspective, placing in view new sites, strategies, and possibilities. As we noted before, social flesh makes the familiar strange in order to look at it anew.

While Tunick's artwork is likely to incline most readers to begin to wonder about potential new political directions, we will very briefly outline just one of these. There is a long-standing assumption in gender and sexuality writings that what has been deemed the private, including sexuality and the sexual body, does indeed have *political* implications (Corber and Valocchi 2003; Beasley 1999). Yet when we look at the literature on social movements and socio-political change, we find that while sexuality is now at least on the table—though still decidedly at the margins in scholarly disciplines like Political Science—sexual *embodiment* drops away. This is so even in relation to discussions of the politics of sexuality—which one might think would unavoidably involve bodies. Embodied sexuality, fleshly sexuality in political and strategic thinking, seems to dematerialise, so to speak. Bodies remain somehow out of sight, even in relation to sexuality. In this setting, it is our contention that a general failure to consider bodies in considerations of social interconnection/community (even in relation to sexuality) amounts to the reconstitution of a public/private divide in political thinking. Where once sexuality was deemed entirely a private issue and not relevant to Politics, it is now present but at the margins of the public. However, though the dividing line between public/private has moved, bodies still remain private and somehow out of the purview of political considerations of sociality.

Why would the fleshliness of bodies matter for our political thinking and strategies around sociality? Just as we earlier suggested that thoroughly embodied conceptions of sociality have an impact on democratic theory and practice, here too we suggest that there is much to be gained. For a start the matter of social sexual fleshliness might alter our view of social change, which is after all rather crucial to the political. Our understandings of social movements, social innovations and social change have remained focussed upon what is seen as public, large-scale and heroic—for example, upon explicit dissident activism, protest and organised movements making claims on political institutions like the state (Gibson 2007; Johnson 2002). Such a focus at the very least means we miss or underestimate the locations and ways in which change may arise. Here we are suggesting the need to pay attention to the micro and 'private' in political thinking. Our continuing failure to do so constitutes a significant gap in deliberations on change.

Yet if we are to give due attention to the micro and the personal/private, this necessarily involves paying attention to *sexualised* embodiment. Indeed we want to insist specifically on the contribution of libidinal bodies to fleshly sociality. To fully recognise this contribution can provide a rather different perspective on what counts in relation to the political and to social change. Attention to the body, and specifically to the libidinal body, can of course offer less usual insights for theoretical and practical debates in International Studies regarding *macro* social inequalities and social change—such as those arising in varying analyses of global sex trafficking (see for instance, Doeszema 2010; Monzini 2005). Importantly, however, we also want to highlight how attention to the (libidinal) body facilitates teasing out how social change might arise at the *micro-social* level and in spaces/discourses/practices not normally understood as political (see Cooper 2009, 2007; Thomson 2011, 2008).

Tunick - Sydney Opera House installation.

For example, how can we consider the problems and possibilities of dominant forms of heterosexual masculinity and how can we identify and encourage forms of masculinity that are productive of global (sexual and gender) justice, if we do not look at citizen *bodies*? We mention this because there is significant existing research in several countries throughout the world indicating that recognition of physical pleasure in sexual health programs has resulted in increased use of condoms by men, and indeed greater involvement of women in negotiation of heterosexual practices. (Philpott et al. 2006; Ingham 2005; The Pleasure Project: <http://www.thepleasureproject.org/>; Holland et al. 1992). Recognition of bodily pleasure in the instance of sexual health campaigns intriguingly appears to produce more egalitarian rather than non-consensual sexual relations between men and women. It is here that we see the terminology of social flesh as opening up what is almost invariably hidden from view and in the process offering new policy directions.

Conclusion

In sum, our joint work on the political ethic of social flesh asks, 'what if we were to *start* from the levelling meaning of a shared fleshly sociality in terms of reconceiving political thinking?' What if the fleshly sociality that Tunick's artworks bring to light was how we *evaluated* political practices and political objectives, including national/international objectives? What if this was what we thought about while generating a *desirable political imaginary*, a model for a desirable democratic polity? Trust and care are not enough. Deliberative and radical models of democracy seem to us decidedly limited.

Social flesh is our shorthand way of proposing a different agenda, a different way of undertaking research, analysis and policy development. We hope it suggests some possibilities to readers too.

References

Bacchi, C. and C. Beasley (2002) 'Citizen Bodies: Is embodied citizenship a contradiction in terms?', *Critical Social Policy*, 22 (2): 324-352.
—— (2004) 'Moving Beyond Care and/or Trust: An ethic of social flesh', Paper presented at the Australian Political Science Association Conference, Adelaide, 29 September-1 October.
—— (2005a) 'Reproductive Technology and the Political Limits of Care' in M. Shildrick and R. Mytikiuk (eds) *Ethics of the Body: Postconventional approaches*, MIT Press.
—— (2005b) 'The Limits of Trust and Respect: Rethinking dependency', *Social Alternatives*, 24 (4): 55-61.
Bacchi, C. and J. Eveline (2010) *Mainstreaming Politics: Gendering practices and feminist theory*, Adelaide: University of Adelaide Press.

Bartlett, A. (2000) 'Thinking Through Breasts: Writing maternity', *Feminist Theory* 1 (2): 173-188.
Bauman, Z. (1993) *Postmodern Ethics*, Oxford and Cambridge: Blackwell.
Beasley, C. (1999) *What is Feminism?: An Introduction to Feminist Theory*, London and New York: Sage.
Beasley, C. and C. Bacchi (2000) 'Citizen Bodies: Embodying citizens - a feminist analysis', *International Feminist Journal of Politics*, 2 (3): 337-358.
—— (2005) 'The Political Limits of "Care" in Re-imagining Interconnection / Community and An Ethical Future', *Australian Feminist Studies*, 20 (46): 49-64.
—— (2007) 'Envisaging a New Politics for an Ethical Future: Beyond trust, care and generosity—towards an ethic of "social flesh"', *Feminist Theory*, 8 (3): 279-298.
Brown, B. (2009) 'Procedure Committee Reference', Parliamentary Debates, *Senate Hansard*, 22 June, 3907-3910.
Connolly, W. (1993) *The Terms of Political Discourse*, (3rd edn), Oxford: Blackwell.
—— (1995) *The Ethos of Pluralization*, Vol. I, Minneapolis: University of Minnesota Press.
Cooper, D. (2009) 'Caring for Sex: The power of attentive action in forging feminist space', *Signs*, 35 (1): 105-130.
—— (2007) '"Well, You Go There To Get Off": Visiting feminist care ethics through a Women's Bathhouse', *Feminist Theory*, 8 (3): 243-262.
Corber, R. and S. Valocchi (eds) (2003) *Queer Studies: An interdisciplinary reader*, Malden, MA, Oxford, Melbourne and Berlin: Blackwell.
Dean, M. (1997) 'Sociology After Society', in D. Owen (ed.), *Sociology after Postmodernism*, London and Thousand Oaks: Sage.
Doeszema, J. (2010) *Sex Slaves and Discourse Masters: The construction of trafficking*, London: Zed Books.
Douglas-Fairhurst, R. (2011) Review of *A Brief History of Nakedness* by Philip Carr-Gomm, *The Telegraph*, 2 May. Available HTTP: <http://www.telegraph.co.uk/culture/books/bookreviews/7771639/A-Brief-History-of-Nakedness-by-Philip-Carr-Gomm-review.html> (accessed May 2011).
Evans, I. (2009) 'Procedure Committee Reference', Parliamentary Debates, *Senate Hansard*, Australian Government, Canberra, 22 June, 3907.
Fischer, F. (2003) *Reframing Public Policy: Discursive practices and deliberative practice*, Oxford: Oxford University Press.
Fukuyama, R. (1995) *Trust: The Social Virtues and the Creation of Prosperity*, London: Hamish Hamilton.
Gibson, S. (2007) 'The Language of the Right: Sex education debates in South Australia', *Sex Education*, 7(3) August: 239-250.
Grosz, E. (1987) 'Notes towards a Corporeal Feminism', *Australian Feminist Studies*, 5: 1-16.
—— (1994) *Volatile Bodies: Toward a corporeal feminism*, Sydney: Allen and Unwin.
—— (1996) *Space, Time and Perversion: Essays on the politics of the body*, New York: Routledge.
Habermas, J. (1979) *Communication and the Evolution of Society*, Trans. T. McCarthy, London: Heinemann Educational.

—— (1990) *Moral Consciousness and Communicative Action*, Trans. C. Lenhardt and S.W. Nicholson, Cambridge, Massachusetts: MIT Press.

—— (1996) *Between Facts and Norms: Contributions to a discourse theory of law and democracy*, Trans. W. Rehq, Cambridge: Polity Press.

Holland, J., C. Ramazanoglu, S. Scott, S. Sharpe and R. Thomson (1992) 'Risk, Power and the Possibility of Pleasure: Young women and safer sex', *AIDS Care* 4 (3): 273-283.

Ingham, R. (2005) '"We didn't cover that at school": Education against pleasure or education for pleasure?', *Sex Education* 5 (4): 375-388.

Johnson, C. (2002) 'Heteronormative Citizenship and the Politics of Passing', *Sexualities* 5(3): 316-336.

Kelton, G. (2007) 'Stay Healthy-Hill's Cure for all Ills', *The Advertiser*, 20 June.

Kittay, E. F. (1998) 'Welfare Dependency, and a Public Ethic of Care', *Social Justice* 25 (1): 123-146.

Kulynych, J. (2001) 'No Playing in the Public Sphere: Democratic theory and the exclusion of children', *Social Theory and Practice*, 27 (2): 231-264.

Laclau, E. (1990) *New Reflections on the Revolution of Our Time*, London: Verso.

Larner, W. (2000) 'Neo-liberalism: Policy, ideology, governmentality', *Studies in Political Economy*, 63: 5-25.

Levinas, E. (1998) 'Useless Suffering' in *Entre Nous: On thinking of the other*, Trans. M. Smith and B. Harshav, New York: Columbia University Press.

Meekosha, H. and L. Dowse (1997) 'Enabling Citizenship: Gender, disability and citizenship in Australia', *Feminist Review,* 57: 49-57.

Monzini, P. (2005) *Sex Traffic: Prostitution, Crime and Exploitation*, London: Zed books.

Mouffe, C. (2002) 'Which Public Sphere for a Democratic Society?', *Theoria*, 49 (99): 55-65.

Orr, S. (2010) 'Great Expectations', *SA Weekend Magazine, The Advertiser*, 25 September.

Pateman, C. (1983) 'Feminist Critiques of the Public/Private Dichotomy', in S. Benn and G. Gaus (eds) *Public and Private in Social Life*, New York: St Martin's Press.

Philpott, A., W. Knerr and V. Boydell (2006) 'Pleasure and Prevention: When good sex Is safer sex', *Reproductive Health Matters*, 14 (28): 23-31.

Putnam, R. D. (2000) *Bowling Alone: The collapse and revival of American community*, New York: Simon and Schuster.

Reiger, K. (1999) 'Birthing in the Postmodern Moment: Struggles over defining maternity care needs', *Australian Feminist Studies*, 14 (30): 387-404.

Said, E. (1979) *Orientalism*, (2nd edn), New York: Vintage Books.

Sandoval, C. (2000) *Methodology of the Oppressed*, Minneapolis: University of Minnesota Press.

Sevenhuijsen. S. (2003) 'The Place of Care: The relevance of the feminist ethic of care for social policy', *Feminist Theory* 4 (2): 179-197.

Seymour, W. (1998) *Remaking the Body: Rehabilitation and change*, London and New York: Routledge.

Squires, R. (2010) 'Louis rules in the House', *Sunday Mail*, 10 October.

Stearns, C. (1999) 'Breastfeeding and the Good Maternal Body', *Gender and Society*, 13 (3):

308-326.

The Pleasure Project: Available HTTP: <http://www.thepleasureproject.org/> (accessed May 2011).

Thomson, M. (2011) 'A Tale of Two Bodies: The male body and feminist legal theory', in M. Fineman (ed.), *Transcending the Boundaries of Law: Generations of feminism and legal theory*, New York and Abingdon, Oxon: Routledge.

—— (2008) *Endowed: Regulating the male sexed body*, New York: Routledge.

Tronto, J. (2001) 'Who Cares? Public and private caring and the rethinking of citizenship' in N. Hirshmann and U. Liebert (eds) *Women and Welfare*, New Brunswick: Rutgers University Press.

Young, I. M. (1990) *Justice and the Politics of Difference*, Princeton, New Jersey: Princeton University Press.

9 | Post-structural comparative politics: Acknowledging the political effects of research

MALIN RÖNNBLOM[1]

Methodology—theorising on the methods we use when doing research—is a central but quite often neglected dimension in research. The acknowledgement of and interest in the methodological dimension of research differs, both between and within different disciplines and fields of study. For example, I would argue that discussions and debates on methodology have been more prominent in feminist studies compared to my other 'home' in the academy—political science. Being a feminist scholar interested in comparative politics I have been struck by the difficulties of trying to do comparative analysis differently, differently in terms of challenging the prevailing positivistic paradigm where 'the world' is seen as already there and instead promoting a post-structuralist position where 'reality' is regarded as only understandable through the constitutive lens of the research process.

These challenges have made me question the methodological dimension of research on politics, and especially on comparative politics. They have also brought me to the point of departure of this chapter—that is, methodologies matter and have political implications. I am specifically concerned with considering what a failure to recognise the political significance of methodologies means for feminist research and the potential of feminist research to be transformative.

The chapter is structured in three parts. The first part explains why and how methodology matters politically and situates this understanding of methodology as political in established feminist criticism. The second part of the chapter demonstrates the absence of attention to critical and political questions of methodology in existing comparative studies and feminist comparative studies more specifically. A final section, drawing on Carol Bacchi's

---

[1] I would like to thank Carol Bacchi and the editors for useful comments on earlier versions of this text.

'*WPR*' approach, offers an example of how we might do critical feminist comparative studies differently.

Methodology matters!

The statement that methodologies matter and have political implications is related to the concept and idea of ontological politics elaborated by Annemarie Mol, and also used by Carol Bacchi in her contribution to this volume (see Chapter 10). In combining the terms ontology and politics, Mol points to a position on reality as produced in ongoing processes:

> *Ontological politics* is a composite term. It talks of *ontology*—which in standard philosophical parlance defines what belongs to the real, the conditions of possibility we live with. If the term 'ontology' is combined with that of 'politics' then this suggests that the conditions of possibility are not given. That reality does not precede the mundane practices in which we interact with it, but is rather shaped within these practices. So the term *politics* works to underline this activity mode, this process of shaping, and the fact that its character is both opened and contested. (Mol 1999: 74-75, emphasis in original)

When focusing on methodology, ontological politics means that we as researchers actually are shaping the reality we study, and that this reality will have political consequences. Here, I find Mol's way of using the term 'politics', to signal how the form of reality we address is produced in research practice, especially interesting—both in relation to the field of study that I am focusing on (comparative politics) and the discussion of politics in feminist research that I will address later in the chapter.

John Law (2004) also elaborates this argument in his book *After Method: Mess in Social Research*, where he starts by pointing to the problem with the way certain beliefs regarding the 'overall need for proper rules and procedures' when doing research have been naturalised. Among other things, this supports a certain picture of the world. In the eagerness to find the right tools for doing research, the question of what these tools *do*, that these tools are a part of the research process and thus the research results, is not taken into account. Hence, our 'methods, their rules, and even more method's practices, not only describe but also help to produce the world' (Law 2004: 5). For Law, like Mol, the significance of this insight applies at the ontological level. Furthermore, how the world is conceptualised has political consequences, a 'fact' that demands both reflexivity and responsibility from the researcher. The phrase 'ontological politics' signals my interest in this chapter to highlight the way research methods have productive and not merely descriptive and technical effects.

Elaborating on the views of Law and Mol, I assert that the political implications of research should be regarded as even more important for research which explicitly studies politics. This assertion requires the articulation of the political dimension in all research, a question that will be addressed later in the chapter. Thus, my main argument is that how we do research has political implications—which of course also have material consequences. In this chapter I outline the need to take these implications into account when doing comparative analysis. I see this proposition as necessary in order to advance the transformative potential of feminist comparative studies—both in research and in politics.

Comparison and methodological considerations

Different forms of comparative analysis are an implicit or explicit part of most research. In order to describe, explain or understand we often unthinkingly draw upon forms of comparison as a method. Although comparative studies are undertaken in several disciplines, I have chosen to focus on the scholarly field of comparative politics with the argument that this field often works as an implicit model, underpinning comparative studies in other disciplinary sites. Even though the focus here is on comparative politics, I believe this discussion to have important implications for research more generally. It follows that we all should be concerned about how methodologies matter in our research.

In addition, my concerns regarding comparison are sparked by some positions in the contemporary field of feminist comparative studies. Specifically, I see a need to address the (lack of a) political dimension in this work, in the sense that there is no explicit discussion of the political effects of the research that is produced. I appreciate ongoing discussions within the field of feminist comparative studies which bring to light the innovative dimensions a feminist approach could bring into comparative analysis *per se* and particularly into comparative politics. Nevertheless, I identify a concern to address feminist discussions of methodology in a more explicit way. While a range of important comparative studies are presently underway, not least in the large EU funded FP6 projects (see Mazur 2009 for an overview), I see clear tendencies in this field to reproduce traditional understandings of politics and the political, and hence to dismiss critiques from feminist scholars on, for example, the liberal constructions of politics and its consequences (Brown 1995). These critical approaches, usually branded 'postmodern', are dismissed as not fitting into the comparative paradigm (McBride and Mazur 2010). This account of the boundaries of the comparative paradigm, when taken alongside ambitions to declare feminist comparative politics as a field of its own (described as Feminist Comparative Politics, or FCP), will necessarily exclude those researchers who are interested in comparative methodologies but who wish to challenge conventional studies of politics. Moreover, it will exclude research work which attends to the research process as part of that which is deemed 'political'.

The increasing number of comparative projects (feminist as well as non-feminist), not least in the EU context, demand a discussion of *comparison as methodology* and a scrutiny of the kinds of normative underpinnings that 'go without saying' in many projects. In other words, this chapter acknowledges the work and effort expended in the numerous projects under the rubric, Feminist Comparative Politics, while wishing to raise questions about the underlying assumptions in this work concerning what comparative analysis should be about. My objective is to open up new ways of doing feminist comparative politics by bringing in feminist scholarly work that addresses issues of knowledge production.

Feminism, politics and the political

One of the core issues in feminist scholarship has been to scrutinise and challenge dominant understandings of science and knowledge production. Well before the turn towards post-structural[2] (ontological and epistemological) positions, feminist studies challenged positivistic understandings of knowledge production—not least through defining gender as constructed or produced in different contexts. During the 1970s and 1980s phase of women's studies, scholars in this field were producing new knowledge on the position of women at the same time as they were challenging conventional research methods. This included a critique of what kind of knowledge should be counted as 'real knowledge' (see for example Harding 1987). In other words there was—and I argue that there still is—a double mission for feminist researchers. That double mission involved challenging both *what* to research, and *how* this research should be carried out. In this chapter I expand this discussion through asking questions about the political implications of our research practices.

The initial critique put by feminist scholars towards 'mainstream research' was that it suffered from 'androcentric bias' (see for example Lloyd 1993; Stanley 1997). The researchers were men, and they did their research on men—but under the heading of doing research on people, citizens and society. The pioneers of women's studies pointed to this problematic and discriminatory situation—and they also gave different answers on how to come to terms with it and create a non-androcentric position in research. For example, studies of women's history both provided new questions and answers about history and also to some extent challenged the approaches when researching history (Scott 1988). Sandra Harding (1993) summarises the different 'answers' offered by feminist theorists in terms of three positions: feminist empiricism, feminist standpoint and feminist postmodernism, placing the first position (feminist empiricism) inside a positivistic paradigm, the second (feminist standpoint) at its borderland and the third (feminist postmodernism) in a post-structural paradigm. Moreover, Harding presents her own version of a feminist standpoint position where she defends the need for 'strong objectivity' as an answer to the positivistic position on objectivity. Harding regards the latter position as simplistic given its focus on the context of justification—that is, it presumed that for research to 'reveal reality' it was enough to 'stick to the correct method'. Her argument for strong objectivity is related to what she regarded as one of the most problematic features in a positivistic position—the failure to acknowledge the context of discovery. According to Harding, not only the object of research but also the researchers themselves and how they formulate the study at hand need to be scrutinised in the research process (Harding 1993).

---

[2] I earlier used the term 'post-modern' rather than 'post-structural'. This use of 'post-modern' is not mine. It is the term used by the feminist comparative scholars to which I refer and by Sandra Harding. Although the terms post-modernism and post-structuralism often are used interchangeably, I prefer to use the term post-structuralism. I see this term as more related to a position in knowledge production, while I regard post-modernism as a broader term where changes in architecture and art, amongst other fields of enquiry, are also included.

In her work, Harding shows she is aware of the critique against 'objective knowledge', a term which carries with it all the traditional and positivistic assumptions. Nevertheless, she argues that 'The notion of objectivity has valuable political and intellectual histories' (Harding 1993: 72). Thus she insists on it being meaningful to retain a position on knowledge as objective, not least because the objectivists otherwise would simply maintain their privileged position. I do not agree with Harding's view that knowledge should be seen as objective. While her intervention in this discussion highlights the normative assumptions in mainstream research, the concept of objectivity constitutes reality as being unassailably 'already there' instead of acknowledging the role of the research process in shaping how reality is perceived. That is to say, the idea of strong objectivity ignores the inherently political character of research.

I would rather Harding had expanded on her evocative discussion of reflexivity as a tool for situating ourselves as researchers, which more successfully brings to the surface the political dimensions in and of research. When discussing strong objectivity Harding argues that this position requires what could be thought of as 'strong reflexivity' (1993: 69), meaning that what she calls the 'subject' of knowledge—the researcher—is part of all aspects of the research process. This argument may be linked in interesting ways with Mol's position on ontological politics. Strong reflexivity in this context highlights, as Mol notes, the *active* constitutive role of research itself shaping how 'reality' is understood.

The concern with reflexivity also ties into (ongoing) discussions in feminist knowledge production with regard to situating the researcher as an active subject in the research process (Haraway 1991). To see research as a result of a joint endeavour between the researcher and the 'object' of research is one important contribution made by feminist scholars. Changing the subject position of the researched object was in itself regarded as a political endeavour, often discussed in terms of emancipation (Acker et al. 1991). Accordingly feminist scholars have argued for seeing research as a way of changing the gendered power relations that they (we) study. Bringing in the notion of ontological politics is to be seen as a way of expanding this emancipatory dimension of feminist research in order to acknowledge that research is inherently political. However, to do this demands a more thorough discussion of the meaning of 'politics'/'the political'.

Feminist engagements with the political nature of doing research clearly derive from feminist understandings of politics and the political. These understandings have grown out of a feminist critique of the dominant liberal/pluralistic theoretical discourse on politics, a discourse that still prevails in mainstream analysis of politics. Feminists have challenged the definition of politics as dichotomous, as creating a border between the 'what' that counts as politics and the 'what' that does not, as well as the focus on established political institutions. For instance, feminist scholars have pointed to the importance of relating the position of women in the so-called private sphere to women's position in the labour market and in decision-making bodies in order to understand gendered subordination (Philips 1991). The feminist critique also involves challenging the position that research on politics in itself is not political.

The argument that research is inherently political returns us to the starting point of this chapter, that methodologies matter. Insofar as I am arguing that methodologies matter because they are political, this statement needs to be supported by a more developed definition of politics. My understanding of politics is informed by the distinction between 'the political' and 'politics', developed by Chantal Mouffe:

> by the 'political' I mean the dimension of antagonism which I take to be constitutive of human societies, while by 'politics' I mean a set of practices and institutions through which an order is created, organizing human coexistence in the context of conflictuality provided by the political. (Mouffe 2005: 9)

Mouffe stresses the conflictual dimension of the political which I believe to be important on two fronts. Firstly, it is important for understanding what is at stake when discussing the political. Secondly, Mouffe's analysis facilitates a distinction between politics as a field of research and an understanding of the political as the conflictual—as opposition and conflict. Additionally, drawing upon the work of Maria Wendt Höjer (2002), it is crucial to stress that public articulation of a question is not enough for that question to be politicised. Just because there is a talk of, for example, gender equality in established politics, does not mean that gender is articulated in political terms—that is, it does not mean that there are openings for change (Rönnblom 2009). Wendt Höjer argues for three prerequisites to be fulfilled in order for a question to be politicised: it must be articulated in a collective and not an individualistic manner, be placed on the public agenda, and be articulated in terms of conflict.[3] To stress the dimension of conflict when deciding whether a question is politicised or not is a way of highlighting the element of power in the theoretical understanding of politics. Thus, to politicise a question is to acknowledge existent power relations in society and thus create opportunities for change. Here, the political is seen as process, as relational, and 'in the making'. This way of understanding the political helps us to focus on the research process—that is, to focus upon the methodological dimension of research, when analysing the political dimensions of research.

Finally, it is important to acknowledge that the political dimension concerns truth production. Michel Foucault (1980) sees power and knowledge as inherently related and from this perspective all knowledge claims on the part of researchers need to be understood as a way of producing the world and 'truths about the world'. With this in mind, I intend to show *how* methodologies matter. For example I aim specifically to demonstrate what kinds of 'truths' are produced through the conventional approaches of comparative politics, and what kind of effects this could result in. In addition, I would like to offer some preliminary thoughts on how to do comparative politics differently—*without* reinforcing the social/political status quo.

---

[3] The focus of Wendt Höjer's research is how violence and sexuality are—or are not—acknowledged as political in mainstream politics. Thus, the prerequisites whether a question is politicised or not relates to a public articulation of the political. While I do not mean to disregard 'micropolitics', or rather micro-processes of power, this understanding of politicisation places emphasis on how issues 'qualify' as political within the established realm of politics.

Conventional comparative politics

The purpose of this section is to focus on *mainstream* comparative politics, the central presuppositions in this field, and to demonstrate that these presuppositions have particular political effects. This focus means that little attention will be paid to some of the interesting developments in the field within a social constructivist framework, developments that at least partly challenge the dominant positivistic approaches found in what I label 'mainstream' comparative politics.[4] Social constructivist approaches which undertake such a challenge may, for example, be found in the work by Herbert Gottweis (2008), David Howarth (2005) and Ian Shapiro (2002). Their work is almost invisible within the conventional and dominant approaches in comparative politics, and that is why I do not include it in this analysis.

The field of comparative studies is extensive, yet at the same time it is quite easy to discern some kind of 'core' or doxa that permeates the field. The following quotes from mainstream comparative politics illustrate this common ground, starting off with a classical text from 1971 from one of the grandfathers of this field, Andre Lijphart:

> [t]he principal problems facing the comparative method can be succinctly stated as; many variables, small number of cases. These two problems are closely interrelated. The former is common to virtually all social science research regardless of the particular method applied to it; the latter is peculiar to the comparative method and renders the problem of handling many variables more difficult to solve. (Lijphart 1971: 685)

Lijphart's focus on variables and the number of n (the number of cases) as well as the use of this terminology shows quite clearly the basic presuppositions in this field—that comparison is about analysing variables in preferably a large number of cases. Furthermore the quote tells a story about social science more generally, clearly stating the presumed self-evidence of a positivistic position. This quote is useful because it resonates with the conventions in comparative politics that still prevail, 40 years later. These conventions are also evident in the following four quotes from contemporary textbooks in comparative politics.

> [C]omparison remains in many ways the fundamental laboratory for political science. (Peters 1998: 45)

> [T]he comparative approach can be regarded as the 'master strategy' in drawing inferences about causation in any area. (Hague and Harrop 2001: 62)

> Comparison is the methodological core of the scientific study of politics as well. Comparative analysis helps us develop explanations and test theories of the ways in which political progress works and in which political change occurs. Here the logic and

---

[4] I will also be focusing mainly on large-scale comparativists but I do want to acknowledge that there also are comparativists who are interested in case studies. One prominent scholar who raises questions about the more classical position in comparative studies is Charles Ragin (see for example Ragin and Rubison 2009) and he also highlights some limitations with the conventional tradition of comparative politics. However, I would argue that he reproduces the same ontological position as the large-scale comparativists presented here.

the intention of the comparative methods used by political scientists are similar to those used in more exact sciences. (Almond et al. 2000: 33)

Comparative politics involves the analysis of similarities and differences between cases. Are there differences, how large are they, and how could we explain them? (Caramani 2008: 4)

These quotations can be seen as providing examples of the kind of ontological (and epistemological) presuppositions that saturate the conventional approach to comparative politics. First, it seems quite evident that the 'role model' for this research tradition lies in the natural sciences. Testing, ranking, measuring and finding causal explanations are central features in this approach where research is about finding the facts and the right solutions. Almond et al. (2000: 33) use the expression 'more exact sciences' for describing what I understand to be the natural sciences, while Peters (1998: 45) talks about the 'fundamental laboratory for political science'. Elsewhere I have asked why it seems to be so important for conventional comparativists to carry out their research in a similar vein to the natural sciences, at the same time as they seem to acknowledge that this is impossible (Rönnblom 2005). However, to prove the 'scientific value' of comparison seems to be a more important endeavour for traditional comparativists than to acknowledge that their ideal of science production does not correspond with the possibilities available within the social sciences.

Another central presupposition is the focus on differences and similarities, as illustrated in the Caramani (2008: 4) quote above. It is as if differences and similarities in a way 'are' comparative studies. It seems almost impossible to think of comparison outside this box. Moreover, the way in which comparison is presented as *the* (scientific) method is striking. Hague and Harrop (2001: 62) regard the comparative approach as 'the master strategy' and Almond et al. (2000: 33) describe comparison as the 'methodological core of the scientific study of politics'.

What may not be as evident in these quotations is the normative underpinning of the conventional approach they take. The measuring and ranking is performed against an implicit normative backdrop. Or in the words of Kopstein and Lichbach (2000: 27): '[w]e also compare in order to find out what is best'. What is then the base line for judging what is best? What do Kopstein and Lichbach mean when they talk about 'the best'? Of course this depends on the research questions at hand, but there is also a form of overall and implicit agreement on 'the best' in comparative politics and that is Western liberal democracy. This normative presupposition is taken for granted in the same way as nation-states are seen as the self-evident entities of comparison, a topic to which I will return shortly. This implicit normative starting point reproduces a specific understanding of politics and democracy, where traditional institutions are placed in the forefront and where, for example, the nation-state is completely taken for granted, as well as liberal versions of citizenship, influence and change.

In summary, conventional comparative politics rests on the following basic presuppositions:

- that the conventional, positivistic paradigm still prevails, meaning that it is possible to find almost *envy* towards the natural sciences and their laboratory situations

where the number of n seems almost indefinite
- that the ranking of countries produces a dated understanding of politics
- that there is a focus on similarities and differences, not on the research questions as such, producing a lack of analytical interest or focus on complex research questions; instead, description stands in for complex analysis
- that the focus on causality and generalisations and a subsequent commitment to analysis based on fixed categories fails to address how the research process in itself includes a political dimension. To talk about fixed categories is to take the politics involved in the production of those categories out of the picture.

These presuppositions result in a lack of more complex research questions, research questions that start from a more multifaceted and complicated understanding of politics. Returning to the starting premise of this chapter—that methodology matters, it is important to reflect on the political consequences that accompany this conventional approach to comparative politics. In sum, I argue that the conventional approach to comparison produces development and change as linear and rational and sees the world as stable and possible to explain. Furthermore, politics, in these accounts, is about nation-states, (specific forms of) institutions and a correct form of democracy sprung from a liberal ideal that fits all nation-states. Thus, the conventional, liberal definition of politics is reinforced.

To illustrate the proposition that research shapes how reality is understood, I will use the nation-state as an example. Most studies in mainstream political science and in almost all examples of comparative politics presume a fixity of 'nation-states' in order to set up comparisons 'between' and 'among' them. How is it then possible to contest the boundaries *between* nation-states, which is an increasingly pressing and contentious issue (Mol 2002)? Law (2004) points out that by deploying concepts such as 'nation-state' as if they were unproblematic, analysts actually reinforce them. Hence they participate in creating a *reality* of nation-states.

Another important drawback when taking the nation-state for granted in comparative politics is that it becomes impossible to study politics through the lens of governance and governmentality. Studying politics in terms of governance often means to locate and scrutinise informal networks between actors and groups both within and outside the nation-state (Heywood 2002). Taking on a governmentality approach concerns issues of 'truth' production where established definitions of politics are dismissed in favour of a focus on the 'conduct of conduct'. Attention to the conduct of conduct enables a focus on where we are seen to 'govern others and ourselves according to various "truths" about our existence and behaviour as human beings' (Dean 2010: 27). The processes of truth fixing actually govern, such that how politics is defined is also how politics is produced (Brown 1995). Thus, employing the lens of governance and governmentality offers a critique of the conventional focus in comparative political analysis on traditional political institutions including nation-states. The effect of stabilising national states is that we lose focus on other forms of politics. New forms of global politics are left out, such as global sex trafficking and environmental changes.

Feminist comparative politics

Feminist comparativists, as we shall see, have tended to be keen to join, rather than to contest, the 'male' stream. This is somewhat surprising given the feminist tradition of raising questions about knowledge production, noted in an earlier section. During the last 15 years there have been an increasing number of comparative studies within the field of feminist research in political science. In a 2009 article Amy Mazur, a prominent scholar in this field of research, described what she sees as the coming field of feminist comparative policy studies (or FCP) through comparing nine cross-national research projects on gender and policy in Europe. She also introduced the concept FCP in the 1995 book *Comparative State Feminism*, edited together with Dorothy McBride.[5]

Importantly, for the purposes of this chapter, Mazur's 2010 paper, written with McBride, explicitly addressed the issue of comparison. Their subject was the Research Network on Gender Politics and the State (RNGS) project, a project in which they both have been senior scholars. The RNGS project started in 1995, 'as a response to the weakness of an initial cross-national study of women's policy agencies' (McBride and Mazur 2010: 3). The project included both qualitative and quantitative studies of several countries in Europe, the USA, Israel and Japan. Forty researchers from 16 countries have been part of the project team. In their article McBride and Mazur discuss how this project used both qualitative and quantitative methods as an example of what they call 'multi-method research':

> RNGS members shared a methodological pragmatism with respect to research methodologies, arguably the bedrock of good mixed-methods research…Part and parcel of this open-mindedness toward methodology was an understanding that qualitative and quantitative approaches could be useful in developing a systematic cross-national and longitudinal study of the dynamics and drivers of state feminism. In other words 'choosing not to choose' one approach over the other. (McBride and Mazur 2010: 3-4)

McBride and Mazur clearly detach the multi-method approach from any epistemological and ontological considerations. Methods are regarded as neutral tools which may be combined as the researchers see fit in order to fulfil the research aim. While authors certainly can blend methodological approaches, the suggestion that it is possible to 'choose not to choose', to do it all, raises important concerns. Deciding to combine different methodologies that rest upon different epistemological positions (related to different ontological positions) has political implications. For example, if specific political institutions are taken for granted in the analysis, these are also produced as self-evident parts of politics. Choosing not to choose among methodologies is clearly a choice that matters. Such endorsement of a multi-method approach is possible due to an unquestioned acceptance of positivist presuppositions, as the following quote makes clear:

---

[5] There have also been special issues on the theme. In 2004 the *European Political Science Journal* (vol. 3, 2) had a section on feminist methodologies and in 2006 there was a special section called 'Moving to a Comparative Politics of Gender?' in the journal *Politics & Gender*, just to mention some examples.

> The move from the qualitative to the quantitative phases of the project improved the precision and reliability of the operational definitions of key concepts contrary to the conventional wisdom that qualitative analysis leads to better concepts. The dialogue among ordinal regression, csQCA and case studies in the capstone analysis helped us put together the components, like the backup theory, of a new theory of state feminism. (McBride and Mazur 2010: 16)

The ambition to organise feminist approaches in order to make 'everyone' feel at home is another tendency I find problematic. It reflects a view that somewhat contradictory research positions can be welded together to produce useful 'outcomes'. This tendency appears in many places, in comparative studies as well as in other fields of study. For example, recent discussion on different kinds of neo-institutionalism suggests that the varied approaches could and should be joined together (see Rönnblom and Bacchi 2010). Kathy Davis (2009) makes a similar move in her discussion of intersectionality where she argues for intersectionality as a meeting place for both structuralists and post-structuralists. I take a different view, that melding different positions is a way of depoliticising research. In the end, some positions always are prioritised and others are silenced. To say, as Davis appears to argue, that we can meet in the doing of research, leaving our ontological positions 'outside', in my view is a fundamental misunderstanding of ontology. How one sees the world clearly has consequences for all parts of the research process. Yet, in the conventional paradigm, ontological assumptions are displaced from the research process, even as they are implicitly central to them.

The suggestion here is not that the research carried out by researchers like McBride and Mazur and others connected to the RNGS project is 'bad' or 'uninteresting'. What I would like to challenge is the aspiration to adjust the research to the conventional tradition of comparative politics—and the consequences of this ambition. In their eagerness to be part of mainstream comparativism, it seems as if these scholars have forgotten to take into account the feminist research tradition described at the outset. For example—and of great importance—they have ignored the call for reflexivity regarding epistemological and especially ontological positions in research. In other words, I do not see the 'feminist' aspect of feminist comparative studies in this approach. Of course these scholars introduce 'gender' and 'women' in their analysis, but in my view more as added on variables than as an approach that challenges conventional understandings of politics and the political.

There are of course other examples of this trend. In the 2006 issue of the journal *Gender and Politics* the special section called 'Moving to a Comparative Politics of Gender?' asserted that feminist scholars are on their way to claiming the field of comparative politics. As one of the authors, Aili Mari Tripp, says:

> [t]his is one of the most exciting times to be doing comparative gender studies. The field is wide open. We have only begun to scratch the surface in answering very central questions in the field and in contributing to the general literature on state building, the role of ethnicity, democracy, economic development, conflict, parties, legislatures, social movements, civil society, and many other topics of interest. But there are many challenges in bringing greater credibility to the subfield. (Tripp 2006: 261)

This quotation assumes that the aim is for feminist scholarship to be accepted in mainstream studies, that the mainstream is the setting that we need to adjust to. The approach is consistent with the feminist critique from the 1970s that I discussed at the outset, in which existing research was seen as androcentric and thus biased, requiring feminist empiricism to 'fix' the bias. Decades later you would hope for a position engaging with the wide variety of critical feminist postures. A more transformative feminist approach would bring different questions to both *what* we study when we study politics, *how* this is done, and what kind of political implications this brings.

Another contribution in the same journal more concretely shows the ambitions in the field:

> An understanding of the operation of gender within institutions across time and place can be employed as an additional independent variable to test the relationship between feminists and the state. (Chappel 2006: 223)

From the quote it seems obvious that gender is defined as a stable variable that interacts with other variables and that research could reveal this relationship. Conversely, research is about finding out, not having an impact upon the shape of 'the real conditions in the world'.

The 2009 article by Mazur mentioned earlier reveals more about the politics behind FCP. The overview of nine comparative projects Mazur makes in her article is of course in itself a comparison, and it is symptomatic that this comparison in itself is quite descriptive and lacks an analytical dimension. The aim seems to be to cluster these projects and assign them similar or different features and then say something on the research ahead. Normative statements accompany the description of similarities and differences that indicate where the field, in Mazur's view, should be heading. Though she claims to argue for doing both quantitative and qualitative comparative studies, this apparently does not mean questioning the positivistic research tradition. In addition, she more or less dismisses what she labels as 'post-modern' approaches with a focus on framing, discourse and policy content on the grounds that they often reject the 'scientific method':

> This shift is not necessarily positive. On the one hand, the key issues of whether formal policies are effectively implemented to actually change gender relations in society are left relatively unexamined and on the other, an absence of clearly articulated hypothesis, formal concepts and findings may limit the broader empirical and applied messages of the studies. (Mazur 2009: 31)

A central dimension of Mazur's argument is the intention to show that feminist research should be scientific, an intention that seems to bring with it a need to separate science from politics. This same argument appears in an article by Sylvia Walby (2001) in which she critiques the work of Sandra Harding and points to the need for feminists to do 'real scientific work'. Walby's antagonism to post-modern work is clearly enunciated: '[i]s "story telling" really the best that feminist social science can offer? I argue that the feminist retreat from modernism, rationality and science is mistaken' (Walby 2001: 489).

While Walby (2001: 491) claims that 'positivism is long surpassed in the social sciences', she does not seem to realize that positivistic precepts can come in the backdoor when we argue for how we are going to conduct our research. In Walby's article, politics and power are never articulated as a part or dimension of research. On the contrary, her arguments on behalf of 'true science' disregard the political dimension of research as non-scientific. To be able to achieve 'scientific results', feminist research in her view needs to leave the political dimension behind. Thus 'science' is articulated as the opposite of 'politics'. Although I find Walby's argument overall problematic, it is her claim that positivism is long surpassed that I find most troublesome, as well as contradictory. If Walby positioned herself as a positivist (which in a way is an oxymoron because positioning lies outside a positivistic paradigm) her arguments would be straightforwardly open to dispute. However, she claims to be articulating a 'post-positivistic' position at the same time as she is reinforcing a positivistic ontology. In contrast to Walby I argue that we need a core discussion of our ambitions and goals when doing research. This claim follows from the opening proposal outlined in this chapter that methodology matters, that research approaches shape how we encounter reality and hence are inherently political. Claiming that 'real research' is non-political also has political effects.

To summarise, the feminist comparative tradition reproduces the same epistemological and ontological position as conventional comparative politics, and thus a conventional understanding of politics, an understanding that ironically ignores the critical stance of feminist scholars. In my view, this means that those working in the feminist comparative tradition fail to acknowledge their positioning as part of the research and thus miss out on how they themselves shape what they research.

What then are the alternatives? My suggestion is to turn to a more dynamic form of comparison where processes of problematisation are in focus.

Comparing problem representations

In the earlier sections of this chapter I challenged the conventional forms of comparative politics and underlined how methods in themselves are political—that is, that they create both different perceptions concerning what counts as reality and arise out of different political positions. For example, to compare nation-states as if they are homogenous is a way of reproducing the political importance of nation-states and to create them as political objects. In this section I will give some tentative suggestions of a different form of comparison that offers a new position on what to compare and how to undertake comparison.

In this proposal of how to do comparative politics differently, I regard policy as produced, as in the making, and thus I emphasize that there is a need to elaborate a methodology that takes this into account. In this context I propose the possibility of comparing problematisations, building on Carol Bacchi's '*What's the Problem Represented to be?*' approach (1999, 2009, see also Chapter 2, this volume). A focus on problematising produces a focus on 'doing' and hence destabilizes fixed categories. The goal then is to create a dialogue between the identified problem representations within contrasting problematisations. In order to illustrate this way of doing comparative studies I will use the example of how gender equality is produced in Swedish universities.⁶ Through analysing both policy documents and interviews with the top-management of three universities I have studied what kind of problems gender equality policies in the academy are suppose to solve. A more conventional way of comparing my three cases would be to secure both 'independent variables' (for example, the organisation of gender equality policies, the number of women and men in top-management), and 'dependent variables' (for example, the number and context of different gender equality projects), and then do a comparison in order to find out which university is 'the most gender equal'. This approach would take 'gender equality' for granted and fix the categories, or variables, of the study. The political implications would be to reinforce the dominant versions of gender equality produced in the academy, and the effects that they bring. Gender equality in this context comes to mean scoring the highest on the different variables established by me or by the university management.

Comparing problematisations, on the other hand, shifts the focus to how gender equality is filled with meaning in one context. It is the problematisations that are compared, or contrasted, and how these could be understood in relation to other problematisations. To be more concrete, at one university the problem of gender equality is represented to be a lack of quality female candidates, while at the second the problem is represented to be a waste of human resources. A third university represented the problem of gender equality in terms of lack of women in higher positions. Comparing these problem representations, including the processes that have lead to them, made it possible for me to reflect on the first problem representation and (for example) scrutinise how the arguments around quality were constructed, and if lack of human resources and lack of women in top positions were connected to the problematisation 'lack of quality'. When I challenged the 'lack of quality' problematisation with the 'lack of women at top positions' problematisation I could see that quality was as much about numbers (of women) as it was about 'more qualitative aspects'. Moreover, the university managers that I interviewed had a hard time defining these qualitative aspects. Thus, this way of comparing problematisations made me see the 'quantitative aspects of quality' and also understand why quality was difficult to discuss in the interview situation.

This way of doing comparison is similar to conversation or dialogue where the comparative element creates space for distance from and reflection on the different cases. It also destabilises instead of fixes a specific normative representation of gender equality and in that way opens up dominant problem representations for critique as well as enabling the generation of alternatives.

The key is to avoid fixing things to be compared and instead challenge the traditional comparative methodology. The concern is that if you do not have fixed categories you will have nothing to compare. In fact, I am arguing the contrary—that, unless you find ways to challenge fixed categories, much that is crucial to comparison goes missing. In addition, I believe that an explicit focus on comparison could be useful for the '*WPR*' approach. One of the greatest challenges when applying a '*WPR*' analysis is identifying silences (Q4, see

---

⁶ These are tentative results from an ongoing project, *Sustainable Structural Change - Possibility or Utopia?* (2010-2012).

Chapter 1 this volume). What is not there? What is not said? What is impossible to articulate? Through a comparative approach this part of the analysis is facilitated. Through articulations in other settings, the silences in a specific context become clearer.

I am clearly concerned with how many feminist scholars have abandoned a critical perspective to join a variety of mainstream bandwagons, such as conventional comparative politics. In tune with my post-structuralist inclinations I see the need to ask questions about how we have come to this, about how we come to be certain kinds of researchers. Where has the longing for 'real science' come from? Why are comparative politics and some feminist political scholars so resistant to the post-structuralist challenge?

Could the answer be politics? The involvement of researchers as advisors in international communities like the EU is large, and the demand from the politicians always concerns 'good practices'. The way that comparativists rank and measure fits exactly (I would say unsurprisingly) into this political paradigm. Furthermore, the focus on 'good and useful research results' does not only apply to the EU research agenda but is also a central ingredient in the neo-liberal governing of universities today (Bacchi 2008).

Consistent with the focus in the chapter on the need to situate ourselves in research, it is important to be clear about where our analytical position regarding research leads *us*. Methodology matters and we need to ask, how do *we* produce politics? What political realities do our methodologies give shape to? My ultimate goal is to put what is taken-for-granted under scrutiny, to bring to the fore the contestation involved in our lived realities. Maybe this position, at least in the short run, will render less research funding, but my hopes are still high for what critical research might achieve. Methodology matters—and this is an opportunity for researchers, not a burden.

References

Acker, J., K. Barry, and J. Esseveld (1991) 'Objectivity and Truth: Problems in Doing Feminist Research', in M. M. Fonow and J. A. Cook (eds) *Beyond Methodology: Feminist scholarship as lived research*, Bloomington IN: Indiana University Press.
Almond, G., B. Powell, K. Strom and R. Dalton, (2000) *Comparative Politics Today: A world view*, New York: Longman.
Bacchi, C. (2009) *Analysing Policy: What's the Problem Represented to be?* French Forest: Pearson Education.
—— (2008) 'The Politics of Research Management: Reflections on the gap between what we "know" and what we do', in *Health Sociology Review*, 17 (2): 165-176.
—— (1999) *Women, Policy and Politics*, London: Sage.
Brown, W. (1995) *States of Injury: Power and freedom in late modernity*, Princeton: Princeton University Press.
Caramani, D. (ed.) (2008) *Comparative Politics*, Oxford: Oxford University Press.

Chappell, L. (2006) 'Comparing Political Institutions: Revealing the gendered "logic of appropriateness"', *Politics and Gender*, 2 (2): 223-235.

Davis, K. (2008) 'Intersectionality as Buzzword: A sociology of science perspective on what makes a feminist theory successful', *Feminist Theory* 9 (1): 67-85.

Dean, M. (2010) *Governmentality: Power and rule in modern society*, (2nd Edition), London: Sage.

Foucault, M. (1980) *Power/Knowledge: Selected Interviews and Other Writings, 1972-1977* (ed. C. Gordon), Brighton: Harvester.

Gottweis H. and A. Petersen (eds) (2008). *Biobanks: Comparative governance*, London: Routledge.

Hague, R. and M. Harrop (2001) *Comparative Government and Politics: An introduction*, Basingstoke: Palgrave MacMillan.

Haraway, D. (1988) 'Situated Knowledges: The science question in feminism as a site of discourse on the privilege of partial perspective, *Feminist Studies* 14 (3): 575-599.

Harding, S. (1993) 'Rethink Standpoint Epistemology: What is strong objectivity?' in L. Alcott and E. Potter (eds) *Feminist Epistemologies*, New York: Routledge.

—— (1987) *Feminism and Methodology: Social science issues*, Indiana: Indiana University Press.

Howarth, D and J. Torfing (2005) *Discourse Theory in European Politics*. Gordonswill: Palgrave Macmillan.

Kopstein, J. and M. Lichbach (2000) *Comparative Politics: Interests, identities and institutions in a changing global order*, Cambridge: Cambridge University Press.

Larner, W. (2000) 'Neo-liberalism: Policy, ideology, governmentality', in *Studies in Political Economy* 63: 5-26.

Law, J. (2004) *After Method: Mess in social science research*, London and New York: Routledge.

Lijphart, A. (1971) 'Comparative Politics and the Comparative Method', *The American Political Science Review*, 65 (3): 682-693.

Lloyd. G. (1993) *The Man of Reason: 'Male' and 'female' in Western philosophy*, London: Routledge.

Mazur, A. (2009) 'Comparative Gender and Policy Projects in Europe: Current trends in theory, method and research', in *Comparative European Politics*, 7 (1): 12-36.

McBride, D. and A. Mazur (2010) 'Integrating Two Cultures in Mixed-methods Research: A tale of the state feminism project', for the Newsletter of the APSA Organized Section for Qualitative and Multi-Method Research March 10th, 2010.

Mol, A. (2002) *The Body Multiple: Ontology in medical practice*, Durham and London: Duke University Press.

—— (1999) 'Ontological Politics. A word and some questions', in J. Law and J. Hassard (eds), *Actor Network Theory and After*, Oxford: Blackwell Publishing.

Mouffe, C. (2005) *On the Political*, London: Verso.

Peters, G. B. (1998) *Comparative Politics: Theory and method*, London: Macmillan and New York University Press.

Philips, A. (1991) *Engendering Democracy*, Cambridge: Polity Press.

Ragin, C. and C. Rubinson. (2009) 'The Distinctiveness of Comparative Research', in T. Landman and N. Robinson (eds), *The SAGE Handbook of Comparative Politics*, London: Sage.

Rönnblom, M. (2009) 'Bending Towards Growth: Discursive constructions of gender equality in an era of governance and neoliberalism', in Lombardo, E. P. Meier and M. Verloo (eds), *The Discursive Politics of Gender Equality: Stretching, bending and policy making*, Abingdon and New York: Routledge.

—— (2005) 'Challenges in the Studies of Comparative Constructions of Gender Equality, *Greek Review of Social Research*, 117 (b): 235-249.

Scott, J. W. (1988) *Gender and the Politics of History*, New York: Columbia University Press.

Shapiro, I. (2002) 'Problems, Methods, and Theories in the Study of Politics, or: What's wrong with political science and what to do about it', in *Political Theory*, 30 (4): 596-619.

Stanley, L. (ed.) (1997) *Knowing Feminisms: On the Academic borders, territories and tribes*, London, Thousand Oaks, New Delhi: Sage.

Tripp, A. M. (2006) 'Why So Slow? The challenges of gendering Comparative Politics', in *Politics and Gender*, 2 (2): 249-263.

Walby, S. (2001) 'Against Epistemological Chasms: The science question in feminism revisited', in *Signs*, 26 (2): 485-509.

Wendt Höjer, M. (2002) *Rädslans politik. Våd och sexualitet i den svenska demokratin* (*The Politics of Fear: Violence and sexuality in Swedish democracy*), Stockholm: Liber.

Part IV

Looking forward: Still engaged

10 | Strategic interventions and ontological politics: Research as political practice

CAROL BACCHI

The focus of this chapter—research *as* political practice—highlights a long-standing concern in my work with the connections between concepts and theories, and political investments. My particular interest is the ways these investments operate at *non-conscious* (note: not *un*conscious[1]) levels and how they shape or constitute us as particular kinds of political subjects. In my PhD thesis on the range of reasons for supporting women's enfranchisement, I explored the packages of proposals and norms that featured in the practices and textual performances of the women and men involved in the English-Canadian suffrage movement. Of course I did not describe the project in those terms at the time. At the time I was an historian! And so the thesis was titled: 'The *ideas* of the English-Canadian suffragists' (Bacchi 1976, 1989, emphasis added). I have since learned new languages to express my interpretations. Finding new languages is exciting because they add a dimension to existing thinking. They sharpen an angle of analysis that you were developing while making you feel that, in a sense, you may have arrived home. I had this feeling when I encountered the term 'ontological politics' in the writing of Annemarie Mol (2002, 1999) and John Law (2009, 2004)—as I shall go on to discuss.

My reasons for highlighting the connections between research and political practice reflect my personal academic experience and the decision to take early retirement. In the later years of my academic career I felt less and less in control of the direction of my research. I felt more and more that I was acting in the service of 'forces' that somehow were empowered to set my research agenda. I see the move to 'evidence-based policy' as emblematic of this trend,

---

[1] The distinction here is an attempt to move away from a psychological understanding that assumes levels of consciousness. Non-conscious refers, not to an assumed subconscious, but to the fact that, for this form of analysis, neither intentionality nor lack of intentionality is a relevant consideration.

a topic pursued later in the paper. Why did this disturb me so much? Why did it matter what I studied or how I studied it? My dismay at the increasing constraints on my research agenda are based on the proposition developed in this chapter—that *research is an active component in the shaping of different realities* and therefore is, at its core, *a political practice*. Hence, it becomes important *politically* to *contest* the view that research produces disinterested, objective contributions to solving clearly observable societal problems.

Despite the language of 'forces' it is important to note that the kinds of constraints on research I highlight do not signal some form of intentional, sinister *manipulation* of research agendas. The practices I have in mind resist any singular location. Indeed, the challenge is to understand how we all, myself included, have become participants in a research culture that positions researchers as 'discoverers' of 'evidence'. I have written about this elsewhere (Bacchi 2008). In this chapter I want to see what is accomplished by developing a contesting position—that research *creates* realities—a position captured in the term 'ontological politics'.

'Ontological politics'

Annemarie Mol has most clearly explored the meaning and implications of 'ontological politics'. She (1999: 74-75) explains that it is a 'composite term': 'It talks of *ontology*—which in standard philosophical parlance defines what belongs to the real, the conditions of possibility we live with'. Combining the term 'ontology' with that of 'politics' suggests that 'the conditions of possibility are not given' but rather are shaped through complex interventions.

A starting premise is that reality is multiple. This is an ontological proposition, linked to a position developed in Actor-Network Theory (ANT; associated with Bruno Latour), that the reality we live with is 'one *performed* in a variety of practices' (Mol 1999: 74, emphasis added). This theoretical stance is commonly described as the 'turn to practice' (Bacchi and Eveline 2010: 292-94). The argument is that reality does not *precede* the mundane practices in which we 'interact' with 'it', but is rather shaped *within* those practices. Because practices are multiple, so too are the realities they produce: 'if reality is *done*, if it is historically, culturally and materially *located*, then it is also *multiple*. Realities have become multiple' (Mol 1999: 75, emphases in original).

Some might understand this position to mean that actors, in the conventional sense, are the prime movers in this process, that they *consciously* engage in practices that shape their realities. Such an interpretation is not at all what is intended here. Rather, the suggestion is that a proliferation of non-intentional practices shape realities.[2] Who then does the doing, if not subject-actors?

---

[2] According to Mol (2002: 33; see also Law 2004: 159), this suggestion that conventional subject-actors are the originators of practices is encouraged by the use of the term *performance*. To deter such an understanding she usefully suggests using the terms *enacted* and *enactment* instead of *performed* and *performance* because enactment suggests that 'activities take place but leaves the actors vague'. Nonetheless, the language of performativity is commonly used.

Events are made to happen by several people and lots of things. Words participate too. Paperwork, rooms, buildings, the insurance system. An endless list of heterogeneous elements that can either be highlighted or left in the background. (Mol 2002: 25-26)

Despite this enacted multiplicity, we generally experience reality as singular. If, however, realities are produced in multifarious practices, a question arises about how 'singular reality' emerges from this multiplicity. According to Mol (2002: vii-viii) the 'singularity of objects' turns out to be 'an accomplishment', an act of 'coordination': 'Since enactments come in the plural the crucial question to ask about them is how they are coordinated'. Coordinating acts or practices are described as interferences: 'Once we start to look carefully at the variety of the objects performed in a practice, we come across complex interferences between those objects' (Mol 1999: 82).

Crucially for the argument advanced in this chapter, research methods are treated as interferences. Says Mol (2002: 155, emphasis in original), '[M]ethods are not a way of opening a window on the world, but a way of interfering with it. They act, they *mediate* between an object and its representations'. For Mol, then, knowledge is no longer treated primarily as referential, as a set of statements about reality, but as a practice that interferes with other practices to *create* realities.

John Law (2004: 144) offers the concept of a 'method assemblage' in order to capture the many accompanying relations that attach to and produce research methods as interferences. Says Law (2004: 144), a method assemblage includes 'not only what is present in the form of texts and their production, but also their hinterlands and hidden supports'. The objective here is to highlight that research methods involve the assembling of a complex array of power relations and hence are always political. Because the shaping of a singular reality commonly brackets, or renders invisible, the practice of this shaping, an important task becomes identifying the relations that produce 'coherent realities' from multiplicity. Tim Rowse (2009: 38) specifies that, as a result, critical questions include: who is 'in the loop'? 'who is authorized to engage' in ontological politics? who gets to create the categories and practices that shape our realities?

Annemarie Mol's examples are medical ones. She (2002: 81) refers to 'the multiplication of a single disease and the coordination of this multitude into a singularity'. For instance, she talks about 'different atheroscleroses' as different *enactments* of atherosclerosis, one performed in the clinic and a second performed in the pathology laboratory. The former builds its understanding on patient symptoms and the latter on blood tests. Says Mol (1999: 77), these two atheroscleroses are 'different versions of the object, versions that the tools help to enact'. Often these enactments cohere but at times they do not. Mol (2002: 95) explains, for example, how a 'walking therapy', proven effective at relieving symptoms, was de-privileged in comparison to more invasive therapies in the hospital she studied because there were budget cutbacks to the physiotherapy department. As Mol (2002: 115) says, '[I]t makes little sense to call some of these sites political and others science: they all have to do with the organization of human lives and the world that comes with this, and in all of them rules, regulations, ideals, facts, frictions, frames and tension are paramount'. Highlighting the political character of medical expertise, she adds that, so long as 'disease' is accepted as a natural category, immanent within a body, 'those who talk in its name will always have the last word' (Mol 2002: 22).

To summarise Mol's (2002: 6) position: ontology is not given in the order of things. Instead, ontologies are 'brought into being, sustained, or allowed to wither away in common, day-to-day sociomaterial practices'. Importantly ontological politics leaves epistemological debates behind. We are no longer debating the varied grounds for 'access' to 'knowledge'; rather we are focusing on the practices that create realities. This shift in perspective releases us from the dreaded 'curse' of relativism and centres debate where it belongs—on the political nature of reality as we experience it.

The creativity of the social sciences

Tim Rowse (2009) offers a social science application of an 'ontological politics' framework. His specific topic is the relationship between national constitutions, statistics and political claims to nationhood on the part of Indigenous peoples. He (2009: 35) offers censuses as an example of a method assemblage, an object with an implicit politics. As he explains, censuses are not 'innocent', neutral statistical registers. Rather, he (2009: 35) argues, they constitute a *political* technology that shapes *political possibilities*. This is because they rest on certain key (and contestable) assumptions and because they have specific (and contestable) political effects. Most obviously, he points out, a census 'presupposes a territory (usually a nation-state)'. It also presupposes 'a shared understanding of the key terms of the instrument—such as "household", "income", "employment"'. For Rowse, as for Mol, the setting up of what he calls this 'infrastructure' is a 'political achievement' or 'interference'. It is not something natural. It is *one* way of organising political information.

Rowse's (2009: 36) particular concern is 'how different ways of statistically assembling Indigenous populations and cultures are related to different ways of acting on, and being reacted to, by those populations and cultures'. He shows that, within national censuses in Australia and New Zealand over a period of time, Indigenous peoples have been created in specific ways—most recently as part of a population binary, Indigenous and non-Indigenous. Some Indigenous spokespeople, Rowse notes, have found the binary useful in making specific sorts of claims, such as claims to do with equitable treatment of the Indigenous 'part' of the population. It is indeed this Indigenous/non-Indigenous binary that sustains the political project of 'closing the gaps'. Rowse (2009: 38) also notes, however, that such a conceptual framework makes it difficult to defend claims about the coherence of the Aboriginal 'population' as a *people*. This example illustrates that the realities our methods create have complex and unpredictable consequences that need to be negotiated with an eye to specific, on-the-ground implications.

Along similar lines, Osborne and Rose (1999) describe the role of social scientists in the production of 'public opinion'. Their article provocatively headlines 'Do the social sciences create phenomena?' and their reply is a resounding 'yes'. They offer a detailed genealogy of the emergence and evolution of opinion polling and the critical role played by the specific technology of the 'representative sample':

> None of the research aspirations with regard to public opinion could have been attempted, let alone realized, without the representative sample. The representative sample is probably as important to the social sciences in the twentieth century as the telescope was [to the 'hard' sciences] in the sixteenth. (Osborne and Rose 1999: 383)

Osborne and Rose carefully examine the 'lashing together' of other practical and pragmatic knowledges that produced a certain consensus about the legitimacy and operability of the representative sample. In this argument, the existence and acceptance of something called 'public opinion' is the *product*, then, of 'the particular procedures by which opinion is elicited' (Osborne and Rose 1999: 387):

> we can observe that public opinion is something that is demanded by the very activity of asking questions in interviews. That is, the existence of questionnaires and surveys *themselves* promote the idea that there is a public opinion 'out there' to be had and measured. (Osborne and Rose 1999: 387, emphasis in original)

Put in other words, 'the version of the world that could be produced under this description [public opinion] had come true' (Osborne and Rose 1999: 382).

As with Mol (though with an expressed distance from ANT positions), Osborne and Rose are concerned 'to determine the *conditions of possibility* of "social" experience in modern times' (Osborne and Rose 1999: 390-91, emphasis added). They (1999: 392) emphasise that one key aspect of the role of social science in creating phenomena pertains to 'the subjective attributes of persons themselves: the kinds of persons they take themselves to be and the forms of life which they inhabit and construct'. Alongside 'genealogies of research technology' we require, therefore, genealogies of persons, to track how 'the phenomena created by the knowledge practice are, so to speak, actually internalized within persons'[3] (Osborne and Rose 1999: 392). Returning to the specific example of opinion polls, they explain how 'people learn to have opinions', how they 'come to "fit" the demands of the research'; 'they become, so to speak, persons that are by nature "researchable" from that perspective' (Osborne and Rose 1999: 392). This idea—that we come to believe that we *form* 'public opinion'—is not meant to suggest manipulation by some outside research 'god'. It is meant to make us think about things we often simply take for granted as obvious and as non-political, in this instance, 'public opinion'.

The 'hard' sciences create subjects in a very similar manner. For example, in *Sex, Lies and Pharmaceuticals*, Ray Moynihan and Barbara Mintzes (2010) describe a simple five point diagnostic tool, called the Decreased Sexual Desire Screener, made available to general

---

[3] We encounter here, in the term 'internalized', some of the limits imposed by available language. 'Internalized' sounds very like the kind of psychological analysis Osborne and Rose would be intent on challenging. See Rose 1989.

practitioners to assess if any of their patients were victims of Female Sexual Dysfunction. The five questions ask about 'normal' sexual desire and whether or not it has recently decreased. The perspective advanced by people like Mol, and Osborne and Rose, alerts us to the ways in which assessment tools such as this one do not simply tell us what we 'have', in terms of a dysfunction or a disorder. Rather this perspective indicates how such tools have a shaping, or constitutive, impact on who we are and how we see ourselves. Specifically, 'measurement' instruments such as the Decreased Sexual Desire Screener play a role in *manufacturing* new norms of high and constant desire (see Tiefer and Kaschak 2002), norms that can make us feel 'lacking' or 'deficient' in 'libido', for example. My research on opinion polling on women's roles in Britain confirms the creative (constitutive) role of academic research and its instruments.

The 'Mother War'

In June 2009 I was asked to give a keynote address at a conference on 'The Mother War', hosted by the University of Surrey. The 'mother war' (or at times 'the mother wars' or 'the mommy wars') refers to the 'old' 'battle', which occasionally still gets aired, about whether women who 'decide' to 'stay at home' and women who 'go to work' are invariably set at each other's throats. It seems that the 'battle' was currently raging in the UK. I took it as my task to reflect upon the 'reality' of the 'war' and what had made it real.

The media—who always love a good war—clearly contributed to the shaping of the phenomenon. On 26 October 2006 *The Telegraph* heralded: 'No kidding: "mommy wars" are on'. On 6 August 2008 the *BBC News*, drawing on a survey from several Cambridge University academics (see Scott et al. 2008), declared that there was '"growing sympathy" for the old-fashioned view women should be in the home and not the workplace'.

Moving beyond any suggestion of media misrepresentation, I (Bacchi 2009b) made the case that academic research must shoulder some of the responsibility for the phenomenon of 'the mother war'. I started by looking at the work of Catherine Hakim (2000) and her 'preference theory', well-known in Australia for its popularity with former Prime Minister, John Howard. My second target was the book, *Women and Employment: Changing Lives and New Challenges* (2008), edited by Scott, Dex and Joshi, referenced in *BBC News* item just quoted. Importantly, the authors in this book explicitly criticise Hakim and her assumptions. Yet, somewhat surprisingly, I found some shared precepts between Hakim and her critics, precepts that help to explain the 'consensus' view of a home/work divide among women.

Hakim (2000) identifies three groups of women (as ideal types) who (in her view) have quite different 'preferences': homemakers, career women and the 'adaptive' (or 'ambivalent') group, who move between the previous two categories (Hakim 2000: 4, 157). Policymakers need in her view to be 'gender neutral', to design policies that allow the women in these three groups to *'choose'* lifestyles they wish to pursue.

Those who challenge Hakim's preference theory tend, in the main, to emphasise the *constraints* that inhibit women's 'choices' (see for example McRae 2003). This dispute displays a familiar theoretical tension between 'agency' and 'structure', in which followers of Anthony Giddens (1991, 1992), like Hakim (2000: Preface, 12), argue that we live in an individualised world of limitless opportunities due to an assumed state of affluence (Bletsas 2010), and those who are less sanguine regarding the absence of social inequalities (Crompton and Lyonette 2008: 217).

Representative of the latter group, Jenny Lewis (2008: 273, 275) directly challenges the language of 'preferences' and, with many others, draws attention to the 'value-laden' character of the language of 'choice'. However, she ends up proposing that a useful objective for democrats and supporters of gender equality is 'to focus on inputs and to aim for policies that maximise *genuine* choice for men and women in respect of work-family balance' (Lewis 2008: 275, emphasis in original). What is worrying here is that this recommendation is remarkably similar to Hakim's (2000: 156, 169; see also Manne 2001; Evans and Kelly 2002: 54)—that policymakers be 'gender-neutral' and create a plurality of options so that women can have *'real choices'*. *Both* Hakim and Lewis talk about *'real* choices', though Lewis would point out that Hakim dramatically oversimplifies the factors influencing women's decision-making.

In addition, while, among Hakim's critics, there appears to be widespread suspicion of her notion of 'preference', less attention has been directed to the concepts 'attitudes' or 'perceptions' (Fagan et al. 2008: 207), and how these concepts mean much the same thing as 'preferences'. Hakim (2000: 14) actually uses the terms 'attitudes', 'values' and 'preferences' interchangeably. In this context it is important to recognise that the notion of 'attitudes' has a history and that its meaning is contested even within psychological studies (Erwin 2001). Key terms used in social analysis, like 'attitudes', I suggested in the conference presentation, ought to be treated as constructs that play a part in governing rather than as descriptors of some assumed empirical reality.

This proposal caused some consternation. Hakim's critics are social *attitudes* researchers. They build their analyses on large statistical studies of women's social attitudes, such as the ISSP (International Social Survey Programme). In my University of Surrey talk I used several items from the ISSP to suggest that such surveys play a role in *producing* the very dichotomy between 'stay-at-home' mothers and 'working' mothers that they purport to measure. Consider these examples of the types of options made available to women whose 'attitudes' were solicited:

> A *working mother* can establish just as warm a relationship with her children as a *mother who does not work*.
>
> A pre-school child is likely to suffer if his or her mother works.
>
> All in all, family life suffers when the woman has a full-time job.
> (ZA 2004: 129-33 in Crompton and Lyonette 2008: 227, emphasis added).

My contention that these sorts of questions (or 'options') create women who think about themselves in these terms resonates with Osborne and Rose's (1999: 392) proposition that people 'come to "fit" the demands of the research'; 'they become, so to speak, persons that are by nature "researchable" from that perspective'.

Why should this concern me? If women are in fact dividing into 'camps' along these lines, why should I care? You may recall that, in ontological politics, research methods are treated as interferences: they 'are not a way of opening a window on the world, but a way of interfering with it' (Mol 2002: 155). They impose singularity on multiplicity and on contingency in necessarily political ways. The 'singularity' of warring camps of women concerns me and hence I sought out different forms of interference, specifically in the work of Elizabeth Reid Boyd.

Elizabeth Reid Boyd (2002) offers a perspective that *reaffirms* multiplicity and contingency. She is concerned by another dualistic debate that mimics the mother-at-home/mother-at-work dichotomy I have been tracing. She describes how 'being there' has become part of the dichotomous talk around mothering, linked in contemporary discourse to a distinction between 'quantity time' (being available when needed) and 'quality time', a competing buzzword put forward by 'working' parents.

Contesting this view Reid Boyd argues that such either/or 'talk' does not capture the experience of mothering at home *or* at work (Reid Boyd 2002: 466). She draws upon the work of Swedish scholars, Hanne Haavind and Agnes Andenaes (1992), who develop the idea of the 'running wheel' in mothers' thinking, where they (mothers) always have one part of their attention on what is happening to their children. They describe this part of one's attention as conforming to the *cyclical* time of children, which sits in tension with the *cumulative* organisation of time in the workplace. Collision between these worlds creates the need for coping or transition strategies, such as Australian Senator Hanson-Young's 'ritual' of time together with her two-year old daughter prior to necessary separations (Hanson-Young 2009). Concerns about 'being there' 'in case' their children need them, says Reid Boyd (2002: 468, emphasis added), are '*shared* by mothers in their reality and imaginings', identifying a '*commonality between women* that is cloaked by the dualistic framework of the present child care debate'.

Reid Boyd points out that the dichotomy *between* mothers (as in the 'mother war') arises because, in the childcare discourse, the male is constituted a worker/not carer.[4] This discourse, she says, 'operates as both *reflector* and *producer* of the male and the female' (Reid Boyd 2002: 465; emphasis in original). She quotes Pringle and Watson (1998: 216) in support of this position:

> 'Men' and 'women' and their 'interests' rest not on biological difference, reproductive relations, or the sexual division of labour, but on the discursive practices which produce them.

In this context I find it useful to think of the 'mommy wars' construct as a 'dividing practice' in Foucault's (1982: 208) sense of the term, a practice that sets groups of people

---

[4] This is not to deny, of course, that many men do in fact serve in the role of carers.

against each other in ways that facilitate governing of the majority and leave the subject 'divided inside' herself.

Needless to say, my suggestion at Surrey that social attitudes researchers play a role in constituting the 'mommy war' was not received enthusiastically. One of the authors of *Women and Employment* asked me what I expected her to do. Her Vice Chancellor Research was unlikely to be ecstatic to hear her declare that she had *produced* the division among women. Nor would he be happy, it can be assumed, for her to abandon reliance on social attitude surveys, a method associated with 'solid research' and 'defendable' 'outcomes'. In sympathy, I acknowledged that there are of course constraints on what we are able to research and on how to conduct that research. I referred to this situation at the outset of this chapter. My suggestion then and now is that there is a responsibility for researchers to reflect actively on the political implications of these constraints.

As one pertinent example of such constraints, elsewhere (Bacchi 2008) I have written about current funding arrangements and how, increasingly, governments set the 'problems' for researchers to 'solve'. There I discuss the current, dominant, instrumental and utilitarian approach to research where 'knowledge' about 'what works', as assessed against these 'problems', becomes the only 'knowledge' that counts. I note that this focus on 'problem solving' forecloses consideration of how the 'problem' is framed, what the 'problem' is represented to be (Bacchi 1999, 2009a). The space to scrutinise and critique the models of explanation built into designated research questions and priorities, I suggest, is increasingly constrained. Earlier I mentioned that this instrumental approach to research is most clearly exemplified in the current popularity of 'evidence-based policy', as I proceed to illustrate.

Evidence-based policy

The idea of evidence-based policy can be traced back to evidence-based medicine (EBM) in the 1970s. Associated with Archie Cochrane (1972), David Sackett (1997) and Iain Chalmers (1989), evidence-based medicine makes the case that Randomised Control Trials (RCTs) are a bias-free method for judging the effectiveness of health interventions. In 1993 the UK established the Cochrane Collaboration as an international venture to pursue this agenda. The logic of EBM spread out of acute medicine into allied health professions and the related areas of social work and human service practice (Marston and Watts 2008: 147). In 1999 the Campbell Collaboration was established, extending the medical model to *social science research*. Its international secretariat is currently based in Oslo, hosted by the Norwegian Knowledge Centre for the Health Services. The evidence-based model for policy making is now ubiquitous, endorsed in Australia by the former Rudd Government (2008) and popular throughout Europe (Solesbury 2001). As a research practice evidence-based approaches have a strong presence in health policy, crime policy, education policy, gambling policy and media policy, among others (Bacchi 2009a).

Evidence-based policy relies upon a correspondence paradigm of knowledge, accepting the possibility of direct access to 'reality'—a positivist paradigm, which assumes 'knowledge' to be neutral, ignoring connections between 'knowledge' and power. Different policy options, it is suggested, can be tested much in the way of a scientific experiment to see which one works best (has the best 'outcomes'). 'What works' is the catchphrase that best describes its declared intent. This approach to research sits in direct opposition to the proposal developed in this chapter that our research methods *create* realities, and need to be examined for their effects in this light.

I describe evidence-based policy as part of a larger 'problem-solving' motif in modes of governing. The links are clear in the policy domain. As exemplars, consider the *European Commission Fifth Framework Programme* (1998-2002) 'conceived', as the overview description states, '*to help solve problems*', and the online 'problem solving network' for EU Member States, called nothing less than '*SOLVIT*'. Beyond this field I see the same motif operating in approaches to education. In Australian universities, among the 'graduate attributes' that students can expect to acquire through a university education, invariably 'problem-solving' is placed at the very top of the list (Bacchi 2009a: 264). Indeed, I suspect that worldwide it has become a form of commonsense to talk about the benefits of a problem-solving approach to teaching—as if 'problems' are given, uncontroversial, and easy to 'recognise', a position my work (Bacchi 1999, 2009a) contests.

Pursuing my interest in how research practices produce or create us as particular kinds of political subjects, it is important to reflect upon how these instrumental, problem-solving research and teaching practices affect the form of subjects we become—the way we come to think about ourselves and about the value of the research we produce. Stephen Ball (2001: 266; see also Davies 2003: 92) describes how funding-driven research makes researchers 'think about ourselves as individuals who calculate about ourselves, "add value" to ourselves, improve our productivity, live an existence of calculation, make ourselves relevant'. More broadly, the top-down managerialist style associated with evidence-based approaches encourages 'citizens' to think about government as the 'proper' domain of 'experts', producing 'citizens' as (more easily) governable subjects. As Elizabeth St Pierre (2006: 259) puts it: scientifically-based research (SBR) is a form of governmentality (or motif of governing), 'a mode of power by which state and complicit nonstate institutions and discourses produce subjects that satisfy the aims of government policy'.

Where does this leave the research project and researchers?

We return precisely to the position I put forward at the beginning of the chapter—that *research is an active component in the shaping of different realities* and therefore is, at its core, *a political practice*. Hence, it becomes important *politically* to *contest* the view that research produces disinterested, objective contributions to solving clearly observable societal problems. The 'turn to practice' and 'ontological politics', introduced earlier, facilitate this project. They move us past unresolvable epistemological battles to focus on 'effects in the real', as Foucault explains:

> My general theme isn't society but the discourse of true or false, by which I mean the correlative formation of domains and objects and the verifiable, falsifiable discourses that bear on them: and it's not just their formation that interests me, but the *effects in the real* to which they are linked. (Foucault 1994: 55 in Bernauer 1992: 144, emphasis added)

I would now alter the quote to read 'effects *as* the real'. The point here is that references to effects 'in the real' continue to assume a reality within which interferences take place. The position developed here is that interferences *produce* realities. McHoul and Grace put plainly the political implications of this stance:

> if discourses don't merely *represent* the 'real', but if in fact they are part of its *production*, then which discourse is 'best' can't be decided by comparing it with any real object… Instead discourses (forms of representation) might be tested in terms of how they actually intervene in real struggles. (McHoul and Grace 1993: 35, emphasis added)

This is where the 'strategic interventions' in the title of this chapter make their entrance. A worthwhile political project, in my view, is finding ways to shed light on the dynamics I have outlined: i) that research creates realities; ii) that research shapes who we are and how we think about ourselves; iii) that increasingly academics are told what to research and how to research. My work has been *dedicated to revealing these dynamics*—from the outset recognising that 'ideas' are inextricably linked to political contexts (Bacchi 1980, 1983, 1990, 1992), that the political destiny of a reform such as affirmative action is tied to the way in which it is framed (Bacchi 1996), that understandings of policy 'problems' are contestable and hence that it is crucial to interrogate critically the 'problems' we, as researchers, are asked to 'solve' (Bacchi 1999, 2009a).

Is it enough to bring light to bear on the dynamics that produce realities that could be otherwise? Can these sorts of interventions produce change in the dynamics themselves? It seems to me that these sorts of questions install a version of the old theory/practice distinction that I would want to challenge. The key point here is to see theoretical interventions as *themselves political practices*.

Tanesini (1994) makes the point that concepts are not descriptive of anything; rather, their purpose is 'to influence the evolution of ongoing practices'. Theoretical interventions, therefore, have political effects. They shift the ground for our political imaginings. They make it possible to create other realities. Configuring the relationship between theory and practice in this way, Connolly (1993: 1) reminds us that 'to adopt without revision the concepts prevailing in a polity is to accept terms of discourse loaded in favor of established practices'. Pointedly, Deleuze and Guattari (1988: xii) compare a concept to a brick: it can be used to build a wall or it can be thrown through a window.

Some of the conceptual interventions that, in my view, offer the chance to shatter a few windows include:

- 'category politics' (Bacchi 1996)
- 'problem representations' (Bacchi 1999, 2009a)
- 'gender*ing*' (Eveline and Bacchi 2005; Bacchi and Eveline 2010)
- 'social flesh' (Beasley and Bacchi 2000, 2005, 2007; Bacchi and Beasley 2002, 2004, 2005a, 2005b)
- 'unfinished business' (Bacchi and Eveline 2010).

In this chapter, I am adding 'ontological politics' (Mol 1999, 2002; Law 2004) to this list. There are, of course, many other conceptual strategic interventions.

Some might assert that this obvious 'politicisation' of 'knowledge' is dangerous since such a stance threatens any claim to authority in a world that sees the 'real' as singular. The task, as I see it, is to undermine this claim. There is also the suggestion that the focus I bring to bear in my work on contested problem representations leaves us wallowing in a sea of representations, with little precise direction as to the political agenda we ought to be following. The whole point of a turn to ontological politics, as presented in this chapter, is to insist that researchers examine the realities they create and to assess the political fallout accompanying those realities. This hardly sounds like 'postmodern' relativism to me.

Clearly, at the same time, returning discussions of research to a political domain, where they properly belong, does not produce simple criteria for 'evaluation'. We should expect no less than prolonged, heated debate about the political implications of what we produce. I should simply like to see an acceptance of the need for this debate to replace the vacuous pretence of an apolitical evidence-based, or problem-solving governmentality. As Mol and Messman (1996: 422) advise, when formulating a research or PhD project, we ought to consider not 'what we want to *know*', but 'what we want to *do*'. As Mol (2002: 151) puts it, 'veracity is not the point. Instead it is interference'. On this note, I end with a simple but hopeful endorsement of continuing, productive interferences.

References

Bacchi, C. L. (1976) 'Liberation Deferred: The ideas of the English-Canadian suffragists', 1877-1918, unpublished PhD thesis, History Department, McGill University.
—— (1980) 'The nature-nurture debate in Australia, 1900-1914', Historical Studies, October, 1999-1212.
—— (1989) *Liberation Deferred? The ideas of the English-Canadian suffragists, 1877-1918*, (3rd edn), Toronto: University of Toronto Press.
—— (1990) *Same Difference: Feminism and sexual difference*, Sydney: Allen and Unwin.
—— (1992) 'Affirmative Action - is it un-American?' *International Journal of Moral and Social Studies*, 7 (1): 19-31.
—— (1996) *The Politics of Affirmative Action: 'Women', equality and category politics*, London:

Sage.

—— (1999) *Women, Policy and Politics: The construction of policy problems*, London: Sage.

—— (2008) 'The Politics of Research Management: Reflections on the gap between what we "know" [about SDH] and what we do', *Health Sociology Review*, 17: 165-176.

—— (2009a) *Analysing Policy: What's the Problem Represented to be?* Frenchs Forest: Pearson Education.

—— (2009b) 'Mothering and Approaches to Policy', Paper presented at 'The Mother War: Current Trends and Critical Discourses' Conference, Institute of Advanced Studies, University of Surrey, 26-27 June.

Bacchi, C. and C. Beasley (2002) 'Citizen Bodies: Is embodied citizenship a contradiction in terms?' *Critical Social Policy*, 22 (2): 324-352.

—— (2004) 'Moving Beyond Care and/or Trust: An ethic of social flesh', Paper presented at the Australian Political Science Association Conference, Adelaide, 29 September-1 October.

—— (2005a) 'Reproductive Technology and the Political Limits of Care', in M. Shildrick and R. Mytikiuk (eds) *Ethics of the Body: Postconventional Approaches*, Cambridge, Massachusetts: MIT Press.

—— (2005b) 'The Limits of Trust and Respect: Rethinking dependency', *Social Alternatives*, 24 (4): 55-61.

Bacchi, C. and J. Eveline (2010) *Mainstreaming Politics: Gendering practices and feminist theory*, Adelaide: University of Adelaide Press.

Ball, S. J. (2001) '"You've Been NERFed!" Dumbing Down the Academy: National Educational Research Forum: "a national strategy - consultation paper": a brief and bilious response', *Journal of Education Policy*, 16 (3): 265-268.

BBC News (2008) 'Support For Working Mums Falls', 6 August.

Beasley, C. and C. Bacchi (2000) 'Citizen Bodies: Embodying citizens - a feminist analysis', *International Feminist Journal of Politics*, 2 (3): 337-358.

—— (2005) 'The Political Limits of "Care" in Re-imagining Interconnection/Community and an Ethical Future', *Australian Feminist Studies*, 20 (46): 49-64.

—— (2007) 'Envisaging a New Politics for an Ethical Future: Beyond trust, care and generosity—towards an ethic of "social flesh"', *Feminist Theory*, 8 (3): 279-298.

Bernauer, J. W. (1992) *Michel Foucault's Force of Flight: Toward an ethics for thought*, New Jersey: Humanities Press.

Bletsas, A. (2010) 'Poverty in the "Age of Affluence": A governmental approach', unpublished PhD thesis, University of Adelaide.

Chalmers, I., Enkin, M. and Keirse, M. (eds) (1989) *Effective Care in Pregnancy and Childbirth*, Oxford: Oxford Medical Publications.

Cochrane, A. (1972) *Effectiveness and Efficiency: Random reflections on health policy*, London: Nuffield Provincial Hospital.

Connolly, W. (1993) *The Terms of Political Discourse*, (3rd edn), Oxford: Blackwell.

Crompton, R. and C. Lyonette (2008) 'Mothers' Employment, Work-life Conflict, Careers and Class', in J. Scott, S. Dex and J. Heather (eds) *Women and Employment: Changing lives and new challenges*, Cheltenham, UK: Edward Elgar.

Davies, B. (2003) 'Death to Critique and Dissent? The policies and practices of new managerialism and of "evidence-based practice"', *Gender and Education*, 15 (1): 91-103.

Deleuze, G. and F. Guattari (1988) *A Thousand Plateaus: Capitalism and schizophrenia*, London: Athlone Press.

Erwin, P. (2001) *Attitudes and Persuasion*, East Sussex: Psychology Press.

European Commission (2002) Fifth Framework Programme of the European Community for Research, Technological Development and Demonstration Activities (1998-2002), European Commission: Luxembourg. Available HTTP: <http://cordis.europa.eu/fp5/about.htm> (accessed November 2009).

European Union (2002) SOLVIT: Effective problem solving in Europe, online problem-solving network for EU member states. Available HTTP: <http://ec.europa.eu/solvit/> (accessed November 2009).

Evans, M. D. R. and J. Kelly (2002) 'Changes in Public Attitudes to Maternal Employment: Australia, 1984-2001', *People and Place*, 10 (1): 42-56.

Eveline, J. and C. Bacchi (2005) 'What are we mainstreaming when we mainstream gender?' *International Feminist Journal of Politics*, 7 (4): 496-512.

Fagan, C., L. McDowell, D. Perrons, K. Ray and K. Ward (2008) 'Class Differences in Mothers' Work Schedules and Assessments of their "Work-life balance" in Dual-earner Couples in Britain', in J. Scott, S. Dex and J. Heather (eds) *Women and Employment: Changing lives and new challenges*, Cheltenham, UK: Edward Elgar.

Foucault, M. (1982) 'The Subject and Power', in H. Dreyfus and P. Rabinow (eds) *Michel Foucault: Beyond structuralism and hermeneutics*, (2nd ed), Chicago: University of Chicago Press.

—— (1994) 'Table ronde du mai 1978', in M. Foucault, *Dits et Écrits*, IV, 1980-1988, Paris: Galimard-Seuil.

Giddens, A. (1991) *Modernity and Self-Identity*, Cambridge: Polity.

—— (1992) *The Transformation of Intimacy: Sexuality, love and eroticism in modern societies*, Cambridge: Polity Press.

Haavind, H. and A. Andenaes (1992) 'Care and Responsibility for Children: Creating the life of women creating themselves', unpublished manuscript, Department of Psychology, Oslo: University of Oslo.

Hanson-Young, S. (2009) 'Procedure Committee Review', Parliamentary Debates, Senate Hansard, Australian Government, Canberra, 22 June, 3907.

Hakim, C. (2000) *Work-Lifestyle Choices in the 21st Century: Preference theory*, Oxford: Oxford University Press.

Law, J. (2004) *After Method: Mess in social science research*, London and New York: Routledge.

—— (2009) 'Actor Network Theory and Material Semiotics', in B. S. Turner (ed.) *The New Blackwell Companion to Social Theory*, Oxford: Wiley-Blackwell.

Latour, B. (2005) *Reassembling the social: an introduction to Actor-network theory*, Clarendon Lectures in Management Studies, Oxford: Oxford University Press.

Lewis, J. (2008) 'Work-family Balance Policies: Issues and development in the UK 1997-2005 in comparative perspective', in J. Scott, S. Dex and J. Heather (eds) *Women and Employment: Changing lives and new challenges*, Cheltenham, UK: Edward Elgar.

McHoul, A. and W. Grace (1993) *A Foucault Primer: Discourse, power and the subject*, Melbourne: Melbourne University Press.

McRae, S. (2003) 'Constraints and Choices in Mothers' Employment Careers: A consideration of Hakim's preference theory', *British Journal of Sociology*, 54 (3): 317-338.

Manne, A. (2001) 'Women's Preferences, Fertility and Family Policy: The case for diversity', *People and Place*, 9 (4): 6-25.

Marston, G. and R. Watts (2008) 'Evidence-based Policy in the Age of Spin: On politics and truth', in K. Michael and M. G. Michael (eds) *Australia and the New Technologies: Evidence-based policy in public administration*, Wollongong: University of Wollongong Press.

Mol, A. (1999) 'Ontological Politics: A word and some questions', in J. Law and J. Hassard (eds) *Actor Network Theory and After*, Sociological Review Monograph, Oxford: Blackwell.

—— (2002) The Body Multiple: Ontology in medical practice, Durham and London: Duke University Press.

Mol, A. and J. Messman (1996) 'Neonatal Food and the Politics of Theory: Some questions of method', *Social Studies of Science*, 26: 419-444.

Moynihan, R. and B. Mintzes (2010) *Sex, Lies and Pharmaceuticals: How drug companies plan to profit from female sexual dysfunction*, Vancouver: D & M Publishers.

Osborne, T. and N. Rose (1999) 'Do the Social Sciences Create Phenomena? The example of public opinion research', *British Journal of Sociology*, 50 (3): 367-396.

Pringle, R. and S. Watson (1998) 'Women's Interests and the Poststructuralist State', in A. Phillips (ed.) *Feminism and Politics*, Oxford and New York: Oxford University Press.

Reid Boyd, E. (2002) '"Being there": Mothers who Stay at Home, Gender and Time', *Women's Studies International Forum*, 25 (4): 463-470.

Rose, N. (1989) *Governing the Soul: The shaping of the private self*, New York: Routledge.

Rowse, T. (2009) 'The Ontological Politics of "Closing the Gaps"', *Journal of Cultural Economy*, 2 (1-2): 33-49.

Rudd, K. (2008) 'Address to Heads of Agencies and Senior Executive Service', Parliament House, Canberra, 30 April, Australian Public Service Commission. Available HTTP: <http://www.apsc.gov.au/media/rudd300408.htm> (accessed December 2010).

Sackett, D., S. E. Straus, W. S. Richardson, W. Rosenberg and R. B. Haynes (1997) *Evidence-Based Medicine: How to practice and teach evidence-based medicine*, New York: Churchill Livingstone.

Scott, J., S. Dex and H. Joshi (eds) (2008) *Women and Employment: Changing lives and new challenges*, Cheltenham, UK: Edward Elgar.

Solesbury, W. (2001) 'Evidence-Based Policy: whence it came and where it's going', ESRC Centre for Evidence-Based Policy and Practice: Working Paper 1.

St. Pierre, E. A. (2006) 'Scientifically Based Research in Education: Epistemology and ethics',

Adult Education Quarterly, 56 (4): 239-266.

Tanesini, A. (1994) 'Whose Language?' in K. Lennon and M. Whitford (eds) *Knowing the Difference: Feminist perspectives in epistemology*, New York: Routledge.

Tiefer, L. and E. Kaschak (eds) (2002) *A New View of Women's Sexual Problems*. Binghamton, New York: Haworth Press.

Womack, S. (2006) 'No Kidding: "Mommy wars" are on', *The Telegraph*, 26 October.

ZA (Zentralarchiv für Empirische Sozialforschung) (2004) ISSP (International Social Survey Programme) 2002, Family and Changing Gender Roles III, ZA Study 3880, Codebook, Koeln: Zentralarchiv für Empirische Sozialforschung an der Universitaet zu Koeln.

This book is available as a fully-searchable pdf from
www.adelaide.edu.au/press

www.ingramcontent.com/pod-product-compliance
Lightning Source LLC
Chambersburg PA
CBHW051617030426
42334CB00030B/3226